the DALAI LAMA'S
LITTLE BOOK *of*
INNER PEACE

CHAPTER ONE

THE OCEAN OF WISDOM

the DALAI LAMA'S LITTLE BOOK *of* INNER PEACE

HIS HOLINESS THE DALAI LAMA

HAMPTON ROADS

Copyright © 2009 by His Holiness the XIV Dalai Lama
and Frédérique Hatier

First published in French as *Samsara.*
La vie, la mort, la renaissance in 1996.
Translated by Dominique Side.

First published in the English language in 2002
by Thorsons as *The Spirit of Peace*

Cover design by Kathryn Sky-Peck
Cover photograph of His Holiness the 14th Dalai Lama
© Steve Pyke/Premium Archive/Getty Images. Used by permission.
Buddha motif by Rochelle Green

This 2018 paperback edition published by Hampton Roads
Hampton Roads Publishing Company, Inc.
Charlottesville, VA 22906
Distributed by Red Wheel/Weiser, LLC
www.redwheelweiser.com

Sign up for our newsletter and special offers by going to
www.redwheelweiser.com/newsletter.

ISBN: 978-1-57174-844-7

Library of Congress Cataloging-in-Publication Data available upon request.

Printed and bound in India

10 9 8 7 6 5 4 3 2 1

~

CONTENTS

~

~

ACKNOWLEDGEMENTS

This book is based on numerous talks, discussions, interviews, declarations, teachings, and other writings by His Holiness the Dalai Lama. It was compiled at the request of Philippe Jost, director of publishing at Les éditions du Pré aux Clercs, Paris, to whom I am very grateful for such an exciting project, with the support of the Office of Tibet representing His Holiness the Dalai Lama in Paris, and especially of Mr Wangpo Bashi, to whom I extend my warmest thanks.

Frédérique Hatier

~

As a child, I was fortunate enough to attend a teaching given by His Holiness the Dalai Lama. It was based on "The Letter to a Friend" written by the great Indian master, Nagarjuna. I did not understand it all, but at the end, His Holiness summarized the essence of Buddhism in this way: "Try to help others. If you are not able to be of help, then at least do them no harm."

This advice touched me deeply, and ever since I have tried to remember it at least once a day. Now it comes to mind effortlessly. It gives me the strength to address the many difficulties

~

with which a simple Tibetan refugee is faced as he struggles for his people's freedom.

I hope and wish that this book, based as it is on the teachings and declarations of His Holiness, will bring happiness to all beings, and will help to bring to an end the tremendous sufferings of the Tibetan people.

Dawa Thondup

Representative of His Holiness the Dalai Lama

~

FOREWORD

Kindness, compassion, and wisdom. For His Holiness the Dalai Lama, who has always based his daily activity – whether religious, philosophical, or political – on these principles, these are not just empty words.

When, in 1950, Chinese invaders climbed to the still gleaming roof of the world and hoisted their red flag, the young Dalai Lama of Tibet refused to retaliate, and the fight between David and Goliath never took place. Why? Because of the Buddhist principle of non-violence, which the Dalai Lama has never violated despite the sufferings of a

~

people who remain loyal to him after 40 years of occupation.

For many years, the Dalai Lama lived isolated, in exile and without support, and might have sometimes appeared idealistic. And yet, he is the living proof that a man who is good and wise can have a voice in a world that, only too often, bows to the power of physical strength, of wealth, or of insanity. In 1989, when he was awarded the Nobel Peace Prize in Oslo, his message was at last acknowledged internationally.

His childhood and youth were marked by an ancient and traditional form of education, designed to train him as spiritual and temporal guide of a

~

country of six million Tibetans. He became "Most Precious amongst the Precious" in the eyes of an entire nation, which tragically, today, is dominated by China. And, at the same time, he has succeeded in relating to the modern world of the West.

So he has plenty to tell us. About ourselves: human beings who would value peace, if only we took the time and trouble to look deeply into our hearts; about our overcrowded world, where we live alienated from each other; about the Earth and the animal kingdom, which we shamelessly exploit; and about the amazing energy of our minds, which we waste for lack of a spiritual approach.

~

He also talks to us about oracles, rebirth, and the *bardo* – the intermediate state that lies between death and rebirth, all of which is strange and foreign to our Western ways of thinking, but in which the Dalai Lama will maintain his belief as long as science cannot formally prove such things do not exist at all.

He speaks, too, about the law of *karma*, according to which this world is a result of our own doing; we are our own children and not children of a god or of chance. It follows, then, that we cannot avoid our responsibilities, and that there is an urgent need for us to face up to this with kindness and compassion, now that the potential for destruction is more of a threat than ever before.

~

With a pragmatism firmly rooted in the realities of life, he invites us to rediscover fundamental values such as love, respect for all life, and the desire for peace, all of which are necessary for human survival. "If we have to be selfish, then at least let's be intelligently selfish," he says.

Such are the themes of this book. The words of Tenzin Gyatso, His Holiness the 14th Dalai Lama, express a powerful vision and such extraordinary kindness that we hope they will speak to many different people. "Even reading a few pages of this book can be very beneficial," he assures us.

Frédérique Hatier

~

On my origins

I was born in a small village called Taktser, meaning "the roaring tiger," on 6 July 1935. Taktser is in the northeast of Tibet, in Amdo province, which borders on to China. My parents were peasant farmers. On the whole, my parents grew enough to feed the family. In peasant families such as ours, it was important to have many children, and my mother gave birth to 16 children, but nine of them died when they were very young. Of course, at that time nobody imagined that I was anything but an ordinary baby.

~

After I was born, a couple of crows began frequenting the roof of our house. They would arrive each morning, stay there for a while, and fly off again. This is of interest because a similar event took place after the births of the First, Seventh, and Eighth Dalai Lamas.

~

How I was recognized as the
reincarnation of the 13th Dalai Lama

When I was barely three years old, a team charged by the Lhasa government with the task of finding the reincarnation of the Dalai Lama arrived at the monastery in Kumbum. Various signs led these men to my parents' farm, where they spent the night playing with me and observing me very closely. They returned a few days later with a set of objects that had belonged to the 13th Dalai Lama, and other identical objects that had not belonged to him. Presented with each one of the objects that had belonged to him, I would cry out, "This is

~

mine! This is mine!" That is how I was eventually recognized as the new Dalai Lama.

My mother remembers very clearly that as soon as I arrived in Lhasa, I said that my teeth were in a box, in a particular room of the Norbulingka (the summer palace). When the box was opened, it was found to contain a set of teeth, which had belonged to the 13th Dalai Lama.

~

Bodhisattva of compassion,
holder of the white lotus

I am considered to be the reincarnation of each one of the previous Dalai Lamas – the first was born in 1351 – and, in turn, each one is considered to be a manifestation of the bodhisattva of compassion, the holder of the white lotus. Tibetans therefore believe me to be the 14th manifestation in a lineage, which goes back to a Brahmin child who lived at the time of Shakyamuni Buddha, some 2,500 years ago.

~

Very few people indeed have ever been considered in any way divine. Thanks to my role, I am able to bring a lot of benefit, and for this reason I appreciate it. This role is also very useful for people in general, and I owe it to my karma to have been reborn into it. You could say that my circumstances are extremely fortunate. However, behind the idea of good fortune actually lie real causes and conditions: there is the karmic force of my capacity to take on the role, and there is my wish to do so.

~

The Indian monk Shantideva wrote:

"As long as space endures,
As long as sentient beings remain,
Until then, may I too remain
And dispel the miseries of the world."

I make this wish in my present life, and I am sure
I have made it in past lives too.

~

My mother

My mother was without doubt one of the kindest people I have ever met. She was really wonderful and full of compassion. One day, when there was terrible famine in the neighboring area of China, and when many poor people would cross the border in the hope of finding something to eat in Tibet, one couple came to our door with a dead child. They pleaded with my mother to give them food, which she did immediately. And then, pointing to their child, she asked them whether they needed help to bury him. Once they had understood her question they shook their heads,

~

and gestured that they intended to eat him. Horrified, my mother asked them to come into the house, and gave them everything she had in the larder. Even at the risk of depriving her own family, never would she let a beggar leave empty-handed.

~

Loneliness as a small child

Several months after the search party had decided that the child they found in Taktser was the true incarnation of the Dalai Lama, my parents took me to Kumbum Monastery where I was enthroned during a ceremony held at dawn. The period after that was a lonely and rather unhappy phase in my childhood. My parents left, and I was alone in a totally unfamiliar environment. It is very hard for a child to be separated from loved ones. Most of the time, I was unhappy. I did not understand what it meant to be a Dalai Lama, because I felt I was a little boy like any other.

~

In the winter of 1940, I was taken to the Potala where I was officially enthroned as spiritual leader of the Tibetan people during a ceremony that took place in the largest reception room in the palace. I remember especially the first time I sat on the large wooden "lion" throne, sculpted and encrusted with precious stones.

Soon after, I was taken to the Jokhang Temple, where I took the vows of a novice. Reting Rinpoche symbolically shaved off my hair. He was the Regent, acting as the head of State until I came of age.

~

Apart from Reting Rinpoche, I had two other preceptors and three monks who served me: the master of ceremonies, the master cook, and the master of robes. Wherever I went I was accompanied by a large retinue of ministers and advisors from the most eminent and noble families in the country, all dressed in sumptuous silk gowns. Each time I left the Potala, almost the entire population of Lhasa, the Tibetan capital, would try to catch sight of me. And as my procession went by, everyone would prostrate in respectful silence, frequently in tears.

~

The master cook

When I was very young, I was very fond of the master cook. I loved him so much I always wanted to be with him, even if this meant just being able to see the hem of his gown below the curtains, which serve as room partitions in Tibetan houses. Luckily, he tolerated my behavior. He was virtually bald, very gentle, and simple. He was not a very good storyteller, and he did not like to play much, but these things did not matter at all.

~

Since then, I have often wondered about the nature of our relationship. Sometimes I think that food is an essential ingredient in every type of relationship between living beings.

~

On my studies

My life was strictly regulated. I studied twice a day, for one hour each time, and spent the rest of the day playing. Then, at the age of 13, I was obliged to do the same studies as any monk preparing for a doctorate in Buddhism. There were 10 subject areas, of which the five "higher" subjects are: the art of healing, Sanskrit, dialectics, arts and crafts, and the philosophy of religion. The five secondary subjects are poetry, astrology, dramatic arts, literary style, and language studies.

~

My studies were not well balanced and did not meet the training needs of anyone who was to become a national leader in the 20th century. They were based on a routine, but I got used to it. Occasionally I would have holidays, and they were happy times. Lobsang Samten, my older brother, would come to visit me. Sometimes my mother would also come and bring me a loaf of the thick and delicious bread that is a specialty of Amdo province. She would bake it herself.

~

Losar, the New Year festival

The most important festival in the year is Losar, the New Year, celebrated in February or March of the Western calendar. For me, Losar meant my yearly meeting with Nechung, the State oracle, who would offer me, and the government as a whole, the opportunity to consult the Tibetan deity Dorje Drakden about the year to come.

Contrary to what people might imagine, the role of an oracle is not confined to predicting the future. They are approached as protectors and healers, and their primary mission is to help people

~

to practice the *Dharma*, that is, the Buddha's teachings. In the past, Tibet had hundreds of oracles. Many have disappeared, but the most important ones, those used by the government, are still there.

For many centuries, the Dalai Lama and the government have consulted the Nechung oracle. I myself consult it several times a year. And if I continue to consult it, that is because many of the answers it has given me have proved correct. That does not mean that I only follow what the oracle says; far from it. I ask the oracle's advice just as much as I ask advice from my Cabinet or my

~

own conscience. You could say that the Kashag (the ministerial Cabinet) is my Lower House, and the gods are my Upper House. Whenever I am faced with a question that relates to the country as a whole, it seems quite natural to me that I should put the question to both these houses.

~

1950: the Chinese invade Tibet

I cannot remember any particular difficulties
in childhood, but certainly the hardest thing was
to take on full responsibility for my role. In 1950,
I was 15 years old. Chinese communists had in
some ways already encroached on Tibetan territory
before that, but it was in 1950 that they actually
invaded. The responsibility of government filled
me with anxiety. I had not completed my religious
education, I knew nothing about the world, and
had no experience of politics.

~

At that time, the world was focusing on Korea, where an international army was trying to quell the conflict. Similar events in far-off Tibet passed by unnoticed. On 7 November 1950, I sent an Appeal to the UN on behalf of the Tibetan National Assembly. It was never answered.

The situation continued to worsen, so the question arose about my coming of age. Opinions differed, so the authorities decided to consult the oracle. Tension was at its height when the Nechung oracle moved to where I was sitting and placed a *kata* (a white silk scarf, traditionally given as a greeting) on my knees. The kata was inscribed with

~

the words, "His time has come." I was only 16, and found myself leading a nation of six million Tibetans faced with imminent war. It was an impossible situation, but I had to do everything in my power to avert disaster.

I decided, with the agreement of the religious authorities and of the Kashag, to send delegations abroad, visiting the United States, Great Britain, Nepal, but also China. Their aim was to negotiate a Chinese withdrawal. The only delegation that actually arrived was the one sent to China. All the others were refused an audience. This was a cruel disappointment. Had the Americans changed their

~

minds about our status? I remember my sadness when I realized what this meant: Tibet would have to face the power of communist China all alone.

~

On the road from Lhasa to Peking

The Chinese proposed that the Tibetan government should send a number of officials to China so that they could see with their own eyes just how wonderful life was in the glorious motherland. Soon afterwards, in early 1954, I myself was invited to visit China, and to meet President Mao. The people of Lhasa were very unwilling that I should go. They were afraid I might never be allowed to come back, or even that there might be an attempt on my life. But I had no fear. So I left, accompanied by some 500 people including my family, my two preceptors, and the Kashag. The journey to Peking is 3,000 miles.

In 1954, there were no transport links between the two countries. For our first staging post I had chosen Ganden Monastery, about 37 miles outside Lhasa, which I was really keen to visit and where I spent several days. As I was about to leave, I was surprised to notice that, without any possible doubt, a buffalo-headed statue representing a deity that protects Tibet had moved. The first time I had seen it, it was looking quite submissively down at the ground, and now its head was facing east with a very ferocious expression. Similarly, I learned once I was in exile that at the time I left the country, one of the walls in Ganden Monastery turned the color of blood.

The Panchen Lama

Like the Dalai Lamas, the Panchen Lamas are high incarnates. The Panchen Lama is a spiritual leader, second only to the Dalai Lama in religious authority. They never held any secular authority.

The Panchen Lama joined us at Sian. He was 16 years old and had grown up in an almost hopelessly complicated situation. There had been a rift between our two immediate predecessors. The previous Panchen Lama had spent part of his life in a frontier region under Chinese control and had died there. The Chinese had presented

~

a candidate from the territory they ruled, while two candidates had been discovered in Tibet itself. Negotiations took place, but gradually the Chinese candidate came to be accepted as the true incarnation. He was then 11 or 12 years old.

Of course, the whole of his education and training was subject to Chinese influence, first under Chang Kai-shek and then under the Communists. It has certainly been an advantage to them to have a Tibetan religious leader in whose name they can make their proclamations.

~

If he and his followers had been able to support the Tibetan cause, Tibet's disaster might have been less complete. But the Panchen Lama cannot be personally blamed. No boy who grew up under such concentrated, constant foreign influence could possibly retain his own free will.

~

Meeting President Mao

During my first visit to China, we were welcomed by the Prime Minister and the Vice President of the Popular Republic, Chou En-lai and Chu Te. Both were very cordial. Two or three days later, if my memory serves me right, I met President Mao for the first time. It was a public meeting. Our hosts were extremely strict about etiquette. Their anxiety was contagious, and soon we were all panicking. However, President Mao himself seemed relaxed and completely at ease. His appearance gave no sign of his intellectual power. And yet, when we shook hands, I sensed that he had tremendous

~

magnetism. Not only was he cordial, but remark-ably spontaneous.

We met at least a dozen times. I found him very impressive. Just physically, he was extraordinary. He had a dark complexion, but at the same time his skin was shiny. His hands were equally shiny and I immediately noticed how beautiful they were – perfect fingers, and an exquisite thumb. He was slow in his movements, and slower still in speech. He was sparing of words, and spoke in short sentences, each full of meaning and usually clear and precise. The way he was dressed contrasted with his behavior: all his clothes appeared threadbare. His dress differed from that of the common Chinese people only by being of a slightly different shade of blue. His whole bearing breathed a natural authority, and his very presence imposed respect.

Apart from Mao, I would meet regularly with Chou En-lai and Liu Shao-chi. While Liu was calm and serious, Chou was extremely polite, courteous, and suave; so extremely polite, in fact, as to make one wonder whether he could be trusted. I realized he was very clever and shrewd.

~

Khrushchev, Bulganin, and Pandit Nehru

During the celebrations for the Chinese National Day, I had the privilege to meet Khrushchev and Bulganin. They did not leave much of an impression on me. In any case, much less so than Pandit Nehru who came to Peking while I was there. From a distance he seemed very affable, easily finding something to say to everyone. But when it was my turn to shake his hand, he grew rigid. He was speechless and gazed into the distance. I was very disappointed, because I would have liked to ask him whether there was anything India could do to help Tibet.

~

Marxism

In another private meeting, Mao said to me, "Tibet is a great country. You have a glorious history. Many years ago, you even conquered a considerable part of China. But now you have fallen behind, and we would like to help you catch up." I hardly dared believe it, but he really did seem sincere. The idea of real cooperation with China excited me. The more I reflected on Marxism, the more qualities I found in it. It was a system that wanted justice and equality for all, a panacea for the sufferings of our world. The only weakness I could find in it at that time was the way it

~

emphasized only the material side of human existence. In the winter of 1954, I and my entourage began a long journey across China, which was supposed to enable us to admire the wonders of material and industrial progress. I greatly admired what the Communists had achieved, especially in the area of heavy industry. I could not wait to see my own country make similar progress.

When one learns about the life of Karl Marx, and the precise origins of Marxism, one realizes that Marx endured enormous suffering throughout his life, and never gave up his struggle to overthrow

~

the bourgeoisie. His vision of the world was based on confrontation. It is on account of this primary motivation that the entire Communist movement has failed. If the motivating principle had been compassion and altruism, things would have turned out very differently.

~

Mao's advice

We met for the last time in the spring of 1955. Mao wanted to offer me his advice on how to govern before I went back to Tibet. He explained how to organize meetings, how to know what other people are thinking, and how to make decisions on difficult issues. And then, moving closer to me, he said, "I understand you very well. But of course, religion is poison. It has two great defects: it undermines the race (since monks and nuns are celibate), and secondly it retards the progress of the country. Tibet and Mongolia have both been poisoned by it." I felt as though my face was on fire and, all of a sudden, I was very afraid.

~

Back in Lhasa

When I returned to Lhasa, in June 1955, I was, as always, welcomed by thousands of followers. My return gave renewed courage to everyone, and I too felt a new optimism when I found that the trust that Mao had so publicly placed in me had boosted my status in the eyes of the local Chinese representatives.

I cannot say how thankful I was to be in the Norbulingka again. Close outside its walls, the Chinese military camp still menaced us, but inside, all was still calm and beautiful, and our religious practices continued almost undisturbed.

~

In early 1956, during the Tibetan New Year celebrations of Losar, I had a very interesting meeting
with the Nechung oracle, who announced: "The
wish-fulfilling gem (one of the names given to
the Dalai Lama by Tibetans) will shine in the
West." At the time, I saw this as an indication
that I should go to India that year, but since then
I have realized that this prophecy had a much
deeper meaning.

~

The Tibetan resistance

Something happened in the summer of 1956 that made me more unhappy than ever before. The alliance of popular leaders was beginning to have considerable success: several sections of the Chinese military road had been destroyed, along with a number of bridges. And then what I had feared most actually happened: the Chinese responded with violence. But I never imagined that they would send in planes to bomb Lithang Monastery, in the province of Kham. When I heard of this, I broke down in tears. I could not believe that human beings were capable of such cruelty.

~

After the bombing came the torture and merciless execution of the wives and children of the freedom fighters, as well as untold atrocities against monks and nuns.

I experienced all of this during my teenage years and my early adulthood: yes, all the measures of oppression, and all kinds of atrocities – monasteries destroyed, works of art defaced, crucifixions, vivisections, dismembering, disemboweling, and tongues pulled out. All of this made collaboration impossible. We went through all these horrors on our own soil. Finally, I became convinced that Mao was nothing more than a "destroyer of the Dharma."

~

The difficulty of being both spiritual
and temporal leader in times of war

The situation was desperate. All my attempts to arrive at a peaceful solution had come to nothing. We were trapped in the vicious circle of authoritarian repression and popular anger. I grew discouraged. The institution of the Dalai Lamas, which had happily governed Tibet for centuries, had become untenable. In my dual role as spiritual and temporal leader, I was determined to oppose any violence on the part of the Tibetan people, but the Chinese did everything they could to undermine the people's confidence in me. And

~

yet, even if Tibetans no longer believed in their political leader, they should not lose faith in their spiritual guide. I could delegate, even abdicate, my political role, but the Dalai Lama can never give up his spiritual authority; indeed, I have never even dreamed of doing so.

It was then, at a time of deep despondency, that I received an invitation to India, to attend the Jayanti Buddha festival celebrating the 2,500th anniversary of the Buddha's birth.

~

Journey to India

For every reason, political and religious, I very much wanted to go to India. After all, it is the birthplace of the founder of Buddhism, the very source of the wisdom brought to our mountains hundreds of years ago by Indian saints and seers. The religions and societies of Tibet and India had developed on different lines, but Tibet was still a child of Indian civilization. And from the secular point of view, a visit to India seemed to offer me the very opportunity I wanted to withdraw from my close contact and fruitless arguments with the Chinese, at least for a time. Not only that – I hoped

~

it would also give me a chance to ask the advice of Mr Nehru, other democratic leaders, and followers of Mahatma Gandhi.

For a long time, we had had friendly contacts with the British government of India. In fact, that had been our only contact with the Western world. But since the transfer of power to the Indian government, political contact with India had faded away and I was sure that we must try to renew it and keep it strong, as a lifeline to the world of tolerance and freedom. I cannot emphasize enough how isolated Tibet felt politically. So I left Lhasa at the end of November 1956, looking forward to being able to move around freely without having to worry about the Chinese.

My very first visit on my first morning in New Delhi was to the Rajghat, the place of cremation of Mahatma Gandhi. I was deeply moved as I prayed there on the green lawns which slope down to the Jamuna River. I wished most fervently that I had had the privilege of meeting Gandhi in this world, and, at the same time, felt tremendous joy thinking of the amazing example of his life. I saw in him, and still see in him today, a consummate statesman who believed in altruism over and above all personal considerations.

~

Like him, I am convinced that non-violence is the best political weapon.

On my first meeting with Pandit Nehru, I explained to him in detail how the Chinese had invaded our peaceful country and how I had tried dialog with them once I realized that no other nation was ready to defend our right to independence. He began by listening very politely, but gradually his gaze became more and more vacant. Finally he said that he understood me perfectly, but was firmly convinced that nothing could be done for Tibet at present. Nevertheless, I confided in him about my idea of going into exile in India.

~

Once again he gave me the brush off, and advised me to go back to my country and try to get on with the Chinese. I said that I had already done all I possibly could to do that, but the Chinese had betrayed my trust.

Before leaving Delhi, I had one last meeting with Nehru. Things had to be clear: India could in no way help Tibet. He entreated me to follow the advice of Chou En-lai and to go back to Lhasa without stopping in Kalimpong, a town in northern India where I had been invited by the Tibetan refugee community. However, as I insisted I wished to go there, he suddenly changed his mind and said, "India is a free country, after all. Nothing that you are doing is illegal."

Meanwhile my two brothers, who had been contacting sympathetic Indian politicians, and my old Prime Minister tried to persuade me to stay in India. All three asked the Kashag to prevent me from returning. But I did not give ground. I was once more going to collaborate with the Chinese, on the advice of Nehru and with the promises of Chou En-lai in mind. But as I traveled back to Lhasa, I had a weary heart.

~

Lhasa reaches breaking point

The crisis towards which we were inevitably moving happened in the second half of 1958, when part of the alliance of guerrillas besieged a large garrison of the Chinese Liberation army in Tsethang. I sensed that if the population of Lhasa, which had doubled with the influx of refugees, became caught up in the conflict any hope of restoring peace would be gone. The powder keg was on the brink of exploding, yet nothing in particular was happening. I spent the long cold winter nights at my studies.

~

Doctor of Buddhist philosophy

I left the Norbulingka (the summer palace in Lhasa) at the beginning of 1959. When I arrived at the Jokhang Temple for the Monlam festival, at the end of which my final examination would be held, between 25,000 and 30,000 monks were waiting for me, intermingled with the enormous crowd of laypeople who had come from the furthest corners of Tibet. For one whole day, before an audience of several thousand people, and alongside other students like myself, I had to hold my own in logic, epistemology, and the philosophies and scriptures of the Buddhist Mahayana tradition.

~

Many different scholars asked me questions to test my knowledge. It was a hard day, but the examiners unanimously agreed to bestow the title of Geshe on me, the term for a Doctor in Buddhist philosophy.

~

*A thousand-year civilization
exhibits its glory for the last time*

On 5 March, I left the Jokhang in a magnificent procession to go back to the summer palace. My bodyguards, dressed in their gleaming uniforms, surrounded my palanquin, and behind me followed members of the Kashag and of the Lhasa aristocracy, all sumptuously dressed. They were followed by the most eminent abbots and lamas of the country, and finally by thousands upon thousands of Tibetans. A civilization over one thousand years old exhibited its glory for the very last time, along the four-mile road that separates the two

~

buildings. Only the usual contingent of Chinese was missing, and that was hardly reassuring.

~

Invitation to a theatrical show

Just before I had left for the Jokhang, I had been pressured by the Chinese to attend a theatrical show, and without any detailed discussion I had accepted the date of 10 March. When I returned to Lhasa, we learned that the play was to take place in the Chinese army camp, less than two miles away from the summer palace. The very idea of the Dalai Lama going into it for any purpose was extraordinary. No one could help feeling that the Chinese invitation was suspicious, especially as I had to go into the Chinese camp at midday without a bodyguard or escort, which would have been unprecedented.

~

That day, as I was taking my usual walk around the garden of the Norbulingka in the early morning, I soon forgot my concerns in the beauty of the spring morning. Suddenly, I could hear shouts on the other side of the wall: the people of Lhasa were shouting that they had come to protect me. Very soon the crowd was countless, some said there were 30,000 people. When some of my Cabinet entered the palace, I could hear the cry: "Chinese out of Tibet! Tibet for the Tibetans!"

I asked the Cabinet to inform the Chinese General that I would not be able to attend the play. I felt caught between two volcanoes, both of which

~

might erupt at any moment. On one side were my people, unanimous in their clear and passionate protest against the Chinese regime, and on the other side was an army of occupation that was both powerful and aggressive. In the event of a clash the outcome was obvious: the people of Lhasa would be brutally massacred in their thousands.

~

The Lhasa revolt

The following days were horribly confused. General Tan Kuan-Sen spoke of betrayal, and accused the Tibetan government of organizing the popular agitation against the Chinese authorities. There was talk of a military campaign that aimed to destroy the Norbulingka. The crowd was becoming almost hysterical. Should I stay, or should I flee? I consulted the oracle, and once again he gave me the same reply: I should stay and continue the dialog with the Chinese. For the very first time, I wondered whether his answer was really the best course of action. And then on the 16th, I received

~

a third and final letter from General Tan Kuan-Sen. It was an ultimatum, confirming that the Chinese were getting ready to attack the crowds and bomb the Norbulingka.

~

Exile

At dawn on 17 March 1959, the end was imminent. There were rumors of fresh troops arriving from China by air. For the exasperated crowd that surrounded the summer palace armed with sticks, knives, swords, and a few rifles, the Dalai Lama remained the most precious thing in the world. The crowd would stay there until the end, and would die in the hope of saving their "precious protector."

It seemed that the situation was completely desperate. I asked for the oracle's advice one

~

more time. To my surprise, he cried, "Go away! Leave tonight!" Still in trance, he wrote down very clearly and in great detail which route I should take to leave the Norbulingka and reach the frontier. At that precise moment, as if to give the oracle's instructions more weight, two heavy mortar shells were fired near the north gate of the Norbulingka. Together with my ministers, I consulted the popular leaders, who immediately offered the best cooperation.

As night fell I went to the chapel of Mahakala, my personal protective deity. I offered a kata (long white silk scarf) at the altar as a symbol of farewell

~

and stayed a moment, praying. The main entrance opens onto some steps. I walked around the courtyard, stopping at the other end to visualize my arrival in India, and then walking back to the doorway to symbolize my return to Tibet. And then I went out into the freezing night dressed in trousers and a long black cape, my glasses tucked away in my pocket. I slung a rifle on my shoulder, and was accompanied by two guards and my chamberlain. That is how I was able to walk through the gate unchallenged, like a humble soldier. And then my journey into exile began.

CHAPTER TWO

TIBET AND LIFE
IN EXILE

~

Truth is more powerful than force of arms

Since my escape from Tibet, I have been living in exile in India. I was reluctantly forced to admit that I would be able to serve my people better from outside the country. Tibet has been under Chinese occupation for 40 years now. We have nothing other than our determination – and the truth – to help us deal with the Chinese. Despite the brainwashing, despite their use of all possible forms of atrocity and propaganda, despite all the terrible methods they have applied, the truth remains the truth. Our camp has neither money nor propaganda, it has nothing but our own simple voices. And yet most people have now lost confidence in the strong voices of the Chinese. Our voice may be gentle, but it has more credibility. The determination of ordinary human beings will triumph over any force of arms.

Even if Tibet is currently going through one of the worst periods of her history, and even though this is very, very sad, I am convinced that we will come out of it.

We Tibetans love our country and our culture, and we have the right to preserve them. We have strong hopes that the attitude of our great

~

neighbor will change. Past experience has taught us to be prudent, but nevertheless I believe that human determination and willpower can defy external pressure and aggression. However powerful and destructive it may be, aggression cannot stifle the truth.

~

Population transfers in Tibet

One of the most important and serious issues related to the Tibetan question is the massive influx of Chinese settlers into Tibet. If the current trend continues for another 10 or 15 years, Tibetans will rapidly be reduced to an insignificant minority in their own country. This is exactly what has happened in Inner Mongolia, where there are now around three million natives compared with some 10 million Chinese. In eastern Turkestan, the Chinese population is increasing by the day. In Tibet, there are about six million native Tibetans while the Chinese population has risen to

~

around seven and a half million. This problem is extremely serious.

~

Patience and tolerance, yes;
but Chinese domination is unacceptable

Every situation must be judged on its individual merits. The idea of forgiveness and patience does not mean that one must accept any type of behavior from anyone. In the case of Tibet, the term "liberation," as used by the Chinese, belies tremendous suffering. Nevertheless, I consider the Chinese leaders to be human beings, and see them as my neighbors, and as a people with a long history and a high degree of civilization. I respect them and hold no grudge. This attitude helps to dissolve negative emotions and encourages patience and tolerance.

~

However, this does not mean that I accept Chinese domination. I am doing everything in my power to resist oppression, but I never act with a grudge. I think Tibetans find it quite natural to face hardship in this spirit. If we do our best, and if we are sincere, we will be happy if we succeed. And if we don't succeed, we will have no regrets.

Compassion for the Chinese

When Tibetans think about the Chinese who are committing atrocities such as genocide, rather than feeling angry we deliberately cultivate a strong feeling of compassion for them, because they are victims of delusion. Even if they do not suffer for this in an obvious way in the immediate term, sooner or later they will have to face the consequences of their actions.

Even if the destruction inflicted by the Chinese communists on Tibet and on China had been compensated by an equally large-scale program of

~

construction, I doubt that they would have been able to make social improvements since they are not motivated by compassion. In Tibet, where the Chinese have carried out systematic destruction and torture – monasteries have been evacuated, great masters put in prison, and the practice of Buddhism has made anyone liable to detention and even to death – people have still not lost their hope and determination. I think this is because of the Buddhist tradition.

~

We ask only for autonomy

Tibet was independent for centuries. It is so no longer. We have to face facts. We are asking for autonomy and are no longer dreaming of independence. But we wish to negotiate on the basis of mutual respect. Conditions today are no longer what they were in the past, and we are ready to follow the motto of Deng Xiaoping: "One country, two systems."

But Chinese attitudes are not moving in this direction, at least at the moment. International pressure is vital, and that, above all, must not waiver

~

because the Chinese occasionally show they are sensitive to it. Each time I speak in public, or I travel across the world, there are Chinese in the audience. Sometimes I even speak to them, and they are skilled at responding very amicably. This certainly indicates that they share my approach, even if their newspapers accuse me of personal ambition, counter-revolutionary tendencies, and of wanting to restore a theocracy in Tibet. I am optimistic, because the Tibetan cause is a just one, and also because China will not be able to ban freedom for ever.

~

My Five-point Peace Plan

In order to develop greater understanding and harmony between China and Tibet – the Chinese call this the unity of the motherland – the first thing that is necessary to establish a basis for mutual respect is demilitarization. This should take place first by limiting the number of Chinese soldiers in Tibet and, ultimately, by withdrawing them all. That is fundamental.

In order to ensure peace in the region, both peace itself and a genuine friendship between India and China, which are our two most populous neighbors, it is essential to reduce the military presence on both sides of the Himalayan range. For this reason, one of the proposals I have put forward is that the Tibetan plateau becomes a Zone of Ahimsa (non-violence). We know that there are nuclear waste facilities in Tibet, as well as factories making nuclear weapons, and these activities should be prohibited. In addition, the country is suffering from an environmentally dangerous level of deforestation; all natural resources should be protected. Finally, the promotion and protection of human rights is fundamental. These are the measures that I have outlined in my five-point Peace Plan. They are all critical points.

~

The Chinese turn a deaf ear to Tibetans,
but are sensitive to international pressure

When the Peace Plan was made public at the end of September 1987, the Chinese first reacted negatively and treated me as a reactionary. That provoked demonstrations in Tibet, followed by repression. I think China, in its own way, is a very civilized nation, but the only power they know is that of force. They don't understand the power of the truth. At times they have said quite openly to us, "You are not inside Tibet, and as long as you remain outside you have no right to make suggestions about these things."

~

You see, the Chinese are turning a deaf ear to us; they cannot hear our voices. More and more people in the outside world are becoming aware of the Tibetan problem. But since our Chinese friends are rather hard of hearing, when we cry out the only outcome is that we grow hoarse. That is why I made these proposals not to Peking but to the outside world. As a result, China's attitude has been more positive on account of external pressure.

~

China and Buddhism

China is a beautiful country. In the mind of the Chinese people, Buddhism is not something foreign or something new like it is in the West. Traditionally, a large part of the Chinese population was Buddhist. There are Buddhist temples and sanctuaries in China. And I am quite sure that if the Chinese people were free to make contact with Buddhism, many young Chinese would benefit from it. If such an opportunity arises, I would of course like to contribute to it.

Although the persecution of Buddhism has not lasted as long under the Chinese regime as it did under King Langdarma in the ninth century, the scale of the destruction is much greater. Whether we are fully able to succeed or not, it is now our responsibility to restore what has been systematically destroyed by the Chinese.

~

The way of peace

If I were to develop feelings of vindictiveness, anger, or hatred towards the Chinese, who would be the loser? I would, because I would thereby lose my own peace of mind, my sleep, and my appetite. At the same time, my bitterness would not affect the Chinese in the least. If I became extremely upset, that would also prevent me from making those around me happy.

Anyone is free to differ with me on this, but I try to stay joyful. If we want to work effectively for freedom and justice, it is better to do so without

~

anger or deviousness. If we ourselves feel calm, and if we act with a sincere motivation, we can accomplish many things in the 30 or 50 active years of our life. And if some positive results have already been seen from this approach, I think I can say that this is in part because of my commitment to the pacifist cause, a commitment which is motivated by a genuine belief in the brotherhood of mankind.

We are not a very large or powerful nation, but our way of life, our culture, and our spiritual tradition have helped us follow the way of peace even at times of tremendous difficulty and hardship, and have given us courage in our wish to develop love and compassion. When the time comes, the Tibetan people longs with all its heart to take responsibility for the high plateau, which is our homeland, and to transform it into a sanctuary of peace where mankind will live side by side with nature, in harmony.

~

A typical day in my life

When I get up at four each morning I automatically begin reciting the Ngak chinlap mantra. It is a prayer that dedicates everything I do – words, thoughts, actions, my entire day – and offers it to others, as a means of benefiting them. And then, as it is cold, I do a few exercises, I wash, and get dressed quickly. I meditate until 4:30. Then, if the weather is good, I go into the garden. This is a very special time of the day for me. I look up at the sky. It is very clear, I can see the stars, and they give me the feeling that I am quite insignificant within the vast cosmos. It is a realization of what we

~

Buddhists call "impermanence." This is enormously relaxing. Sometimes I don't think about anything in particular, I simply enjoy the dawn and listen to the birds.

Next, I have my breakfast and listen to the news on the BBC World Service. Then from six to nine, I practice meditation. Through meditation all Buddhists try to develop a good motivation: one of compassion, forgiveness, and tolerance. I meditate six or seven times a day.

From nine o'clock until lunch, I read and study the scriptures. Buddhism is a very profound religion,

~

and although I have been studying it all my life I still have much to learn. I also try to read some Western masters. I would like to spend more time studying Western philosophy and science. Occasionally, I take a break and pursue one of my personal interests. Since childhood I have been fascinated by mechanical objects. I mend watches and clocks, and I also like planting seeds in the greenhouse. My favorite plants are delphiniums and tulips; I love to watch them grow.

At 12:30 I have my lunch, generally non-vegetarian. Even though I prefer vegetarian cooking, I have been advised to eat meat for health reasons. The

~

afternoon is taken up with official meetings, with the Kashag, with members of the parliamentary assembly of the Tibetan people, or with individuals who have arrived from Tibet with or without the permission of the Chinese. I am always very sad to hear what they have to say; every one of them has a story of suffering, and they break down in tears.

At six o'clock I have tea. In accordance with my monastic vows, I do not have dinner. At seven, I watch a little television. I like the BBC series on Western civilization, and their wonderful nature programs. Finally it is time to sleep. Before I go to bed I practice meditation again, and pray. I pray

~

especially to Avalokiteshvara, the protective deity of Tibet, on behalf of my people. I go to sleep between 8:30 and 9pm.

~

My monastic robes

I wear the same maroon robes as all other monks. They are not very good quality, and have been patched several times. If they were made of a single piece of good material, one would be able to sell them and get something for them. But in this way, one cannot do that. This reinforces our philosophy of detachment from worldly possessions. Like all other monks, I obey the vows of poverty and have no personal possessions.

~

My religion is kindness

Every action that is conscious, and that aims at bringing about a result, arises from a motivation. My religion is very simple: my key motivation is love. My religion is kindness.

*We have to know how to remain strong
in the face of adversity*

My motivation is to benefit all beings. However, there is no doubt that in second place, my efforts are directed to benefiting Tibetans specifically. When 50,000 members of the Shakya clan were killed in a single day, Buddha Shakyamuni, who was a member of this clan, did not express any pain. He was leaning against a tree and said, "I feel a little sad today because 50,000 members of my clan have been killed." But he himself was not affected. That's how it is. It was the cause and the effect of their karma. There was nothing that could

~

be done. Thinking this way makes me feel stronger and more engaged. It will not do at all to lose one's inner strength and determination when faced with the universal experience of suffering.

~

What makes Tibet special?

I defend the Tibetan cause because I wish to serve humanity. In the 19th century, we were still a peace-loving nation endowed with a unique culture. If we were rather backward in material terms, spiritually speaking we were quite prosperous. We are Buddhists, and the form of Buddhism that we practice is one of the most complete. Furthermore, we have kept it really alive over the centuries. It is not only as a Tibetan that I consider it vital to ensure the survival of this culture and of this nation; it is simply as a human being who hopes they can make a contribution to the world as a whole.

~

The Tibetan character

A peaceful, cultured way of life must go hand in hand with ethical behavior founded on spirituality. The kings of Tibet had developed laws on the basis of Buddhist ethics. Today, people from many different countries say that they find Tibetans exceptionally kind and friendly. I can see no reason for this other than the fact that our culture has been based for centuries on the Buddhist teaching of non-violence, or *ahimsa*.

Tibet is a vast country that is not densely populated. This naturally brings with it a strong sense of the importance of cooperation. In a very populated country, it may, on the contrary, feel quite natural to regard one's neighbor with suspicion, almost as a rival one wishes to keep at a distance. In Tibet, we had a feeling of space. And if to this we add the influence of Buddhism, one can understand why Tibetans also have a characteristically flexible attitude and temperament.

Generally speaking, Tibetans are also known for being joyful. "What is your secret?" is the question I am asked time and again about this. Whether we are educated or illiterate, we are used to thinking of all living beings as "our mothers

~

and fathers." These are the terms that were always used in Tibet. I feel that it is our identification with the compassionate ideal that is at the source of our good-naturedness and our sense of joy.

Although historically Tibetans have been a nation of warriors, fundamentally Tibetans are pacifists. For them, there could be no worse job than being a soldier. In their eyes, soldiers are nothing but butchers.

I cannot say that there is never any violence within Tibetan families. But when it does occur, people are somewhat surprised. It is quite rare. The same

~

goes for divorce. It can happen, but most people react to such news with puzzlement. Traditionally, in Asia, family relations seem to be better than in the West. We place a great deal of emphasis on parental authority, on the family, and on harmony within the family.

Despite the brutal methods used by the Chinese, the Tibetan people show a tremendous national determination. Naturally, sometimes we feel sad. I feel even sadder when I hear that despite hunger and terror, many Tibetans have confidence in me and expect me to help, because this gives me a heavy burden of responsibility. People have

~

too much confidence and expectation in me. I can do so little from here! My action is limited. We do our best, and we maintain a clear motivation as much as possible. Whether we will succeed or not is another matter.

~

The Nobel Peace Prize:
a significant asset

When I was awarded the Nobel Peace Prize in 1989, many people learned about the Tibetan question for the first time. They took out their maps and asked, "Where is Tibet, actually?" The Nobel Prize was a great help in my relations with statesmen. Some felt able to receive me officially. Others, like President Mitterand, received me privately – diplomatic reasons always come into play. And yes, the Nobel Prize played a positive role even with the Chinese.

~

Returning to Tibet

Although Tibetans would like me to return to Tibet, I receive messages from inside the country advising me not to go back under the present circumstances. They do not want me to become a Chinese puppet like the Panchen Lama. Not a single hour in the day goes by without my thinking about the situation in Tibet, and of my people imprisoned in their mountain fortress. When I fall asleep at night, if the moon is shining I think to myself that it will also be shining on my people in Tibet. Although I am a refugee I remain free, free to speak on behalf of my people. I am more useful

~

in the free world as a spokesman for Tibet. I can serve my country better from exile.

I do believe that I will be able to return to Tibet in this life. But that is not such an important question. The main problem is our freedom. Whether I am the Dalai Lama or the monk Tenzin Gyatso, I want to be free to bring the maximum benefit to Tibetans and other nations in whichever way I can. From this point of view, if I find more opportunity to do this outside of Tibet, I will stay outside. If the opportunities inside and outside are equal, then I will go back. Either to Tibet, or to China. My real concern is to do whatever is best. It is pointless to

~

go back to Tibet or to China if that only provokes trouble, or if it does not provide an opportunity to bring benefit.

~

The positive side of living in exile

The positive side of living in exile is that one looks at one's country in a different way. So, for example, when I think of Tibet now, all the rituals which pervaded my childhood have lost their importance. From the first day of the year to the last, life was just a long series of ceremonies, all perfectly arranged, that everyone took extremely seriously. This formality ruled even the detail of my everyday life. One had to abide by this etiquette even as one talked or walked.

~

My exile and everything that followed – our patient struggle to be recognized by other nations, all my traveling, all my speeches – have brought me in touch with reality. I also have to admit that exile has enabled me to discover the rest of the world, to meet other peoples, to get to know other traditions. Nothing could be more valuable.

We were granted asylum by India. Living in a free country, and in Dharamsala, has made communication much easier than it was in the Fifties in Tibet. And since this difficult phase of our history, we now feel more "Tibetan" than ever before. Century after century of living together in

~

one's own country can erode this national feeling. Our connections with the land seem a given, and beyond question. When something happens that does question these connections, you then discover what cynical brutality is, how force can be so crushing, and how fragile you are. When you leave, you see the occupation and ravaging of your country only from a distance, and yet you realize that your land has not gone away. It lives on inside you, and you still feel a Tibetan. And then you ask yourself, "What does it really mean to be a Tibetan?"

~

The last Dalai Lama?

I am sometimes asked whether I will be the last Dalai Lama. That is very possible, for two reasons. The first is above all political. For 35 years, the Chinese have been repeating over and over again that I only have one aim, and that is to restore the kingdom of old, to re-employ all my servants, enjoy all my privileges, and be lord of the thousand rooms of the Potala. I reply that I am not responsible for the institution of the Dalai Lamas. That is up to Tibetans themselves. I have said this very clearly several times. One day, if Tibet regains its independence, or at least its autonomy – and I

~

hope this happens with all my heart – this will only be able to take place on a democratic basis. Will Tibetans want the institution of the Dalai Lama to continue? They will decide. If a majority decides against, I will withdraw. And in this case I will effectively be the last Dalai Lama.

The second reason is historical. Many people think that the institution of the Dalai Lamas is intrinsic to Tibet. That is wrong. Until the 14th century, Tibet actually existed without any Dalai Lamas. The same could happen in the future. So I solemnly state: the next government of Tibet must be democratically elected.

CHAPTER THREE

THE WORLD TODAY

~

Our mundane concerns

Like and dislike, gain and loss, praise and blame, fame and disgrace: these are the eight mundane concerns which condition our existence.

~

History reflects our
understanding

The history of humanity is, in some respects, the history of man's understanding. Historical events, wars, progress, tragedies, and so on, all of these reflect the negative and positive thoughts of mankind. All the great personalities of history, the liberators, the great thinkers, all such people reflect positive thinking; whereas tragic events, tyranny, and terrible wars have resulted from negative thinking. Therefore the only thing that is really worthwhile is to increase the power and influence of positive thinking, and to reduce the occurrence of negative

~

thinking. If you let anger and hatred run loose, you are lost. And no sensible human being wants to get lost.

~

Short-term politics

Many of today's world leaders have great courage: the courage to do harm. They are ill-advised, too clever, or too skillful. I think bad political systems, by which I mean systems that are not founded on a desire for justice, are mainly due to a type of short-sightedness. When politicians see things only in the short term, they inevitably only see the short-term gains. That is how they develop the type of courage that is necessary to harm others.

~

War is massacre

It is very dangerous to ignore the suffering of any living being. Even in wartime it is better to be aware of the suffering of others, including the suffering we inflict ourselves, even though this can make us uncomfortable. War is massacre. It is 100 per cent negative. And the way war has now become automated makes it even worse. And when soldiers overlook another person's suffering in order to make some petty gain, then this is more dangerous still.

~

Inner transformation is the basis for peace

Weapons never stay in their boxes. Once a weapon has been manufactured, sooner or later someone will use it. If it were possible to bring about true and lasting peace by force of arms, then we should turn all our factories into weapons factories. But that is impossible. Even though it is difficult to try to bring about peace through inner transformation, it is the only way of establishing sustainable peace in the world. Despite the practical difficulties involved, and the feeling that this approach is unrealistic, I believe it is worth a try. That is why I present these ideas wherever I go.

~

War and peace

There are signs that our ideas about warfare have changed. Until the 1970s, people generally still thought that when there is conflict the final outcome is determined by victory. This is an ancient law: the victor is right, victory is a sign from God, or is a sign that the gods are on his side. In Gandhi's lifetime, a man I greatly respect, non-violence tended to be considered a sign of weakness, a refusal to take action, almost an act of cowardice. This is no longer the case. Choosing non-violence is today seen as a positive choice which reflects true strength. It has been chosen, for example, by South Africa.

~

It should be possible to reconcile politics and non-violence (*ahimsa*). Looking back at the 20th century, you will see that it developed a wide range of methods to ensure that violence in human relations became the rule. This extends from world wars to the destruction of entire cities, to the holocaust, to the institutionalization of torture, and to terrorism. All these methods have failed, and they will always fail because they are only superficial. They have to contend with the powerful depths of human nature, which is made of goodness and generosity.

Practically speaking, it is possible to attain our objectives through violence, but only at the expense of someone else's wellbeing. So, as we are resolving one problem we are sowing the seeds of another. The best way to overcome difficulties is to rely on human understanding and respect. On the one hand, make some concessions, and on the other hand, take the problem seriously. Maybe no outcome will be completely satisfactory, but something happens in the process. At the very least one avoids creating a new problem in the future.

~

A global family

The world is becoming smaller and smaller. Nations are far more interdependent than before. Our generation has reached the threshold of a new era of human history: the birth of a global family. Whether we like it or not, all the members of our vast and varied human family have to learn to live together somehow. We need to develop a greater sense of universal responsibility, on both the individual and collective level.

~

On the gap between rich and poor

Western countries are never satisfied. They have everything, and they still want more. Other countries, like Ethiopia, suffer from chronic famine. They have nothing, and tomorrow they will have less than nothing. We must act to close this ever-increasing gap, and bring together the developed and less developed worlds so they meet on comparable ground, if not on a basis of equality. Yes, this should be our priority.

All the problems that people have in everyday life – famine, unemployment, insecurity, delinquency,

~

mental problems, epidemics, drugs, insanity, despair, and terrorism – are all bound up with the widening gap between nations. Needless to say, the gap between rich and poor also exists within the rich nations themselves. Buddhism is very clear on this point, and long experience confirms our view at every turn: everything is linked together, everything is interconnected, and this is why we must reduce that gap.

~

The Western outlook is rigid

Overall I have found much that is impressive about Western society. In particular, I admire its energy and creativity and hunger for knowledge. On the other hand, a number of things about the Western way of life cause me concern. People there are inclined to think in terms of "black and white," and "either, or," ignoring the fact that everything is interdependent and relative. They tend to lose sight of the gray areas that always exist between two points of view.

~

For example, if we were to observe our planet from space, we would see no frontiers. All the boundaries we erect are purely artificial. We create distinctions on the basis of skin color, or geographical location, or history and that is enough to make us feel different. That is how criticism and conflict grows. But from a more global perspective, we are all brothers and sisters.

~

On national isolationism

Isolation is never good for a country, and today it has become quite impracticable. During the first half of the 20th century, Tibet had very little contact with other nations and traditions, and this was very damaging. The passage of time left her lagging behind, and that meant a brutal awakening. Some Muslim countries still maintain and even reinforce a sense of closedness. But if we look at the world as a whole, national isolation is less common. Over the last 20 years or so, I have visited many countries and everywhere I go people say to me, "Now, we know each other better."

~

Responsibility for our environment

In the first half of the 20th century, the inhabitants of Earth had no idea of the responsibility they had towards their planet. Factories spread far and wide, especially in the West, spilling their wastes into all the natural elements. And strangely enough, nobody was taking any notice. The result has been a massive extinction of species, the greatest for 65 million years, and for a Buddhist this is an abomination.

In the past, the long-term effects of our actions were less evident. But today, thanks to science

~

and technology, we are capable of bringing about either great benefits or terrible disasters. The threat of nuclear weapons and man's ability to destroy the environment are really alarming. And yet there are other almost imperceptible changes – I am thinking of the exhaustion of our natural resources, and especially of soil erosion – and these are perhaps more dangerous still, because once we begin to feel their repercussions it will be too late.

This planet is our home. Taking care of our world and of our planet is like looking after our own home. In a way, one can say that the Earth is our mother. She is so good that whatever we do, she

~

puts up with it. But now the time has come when our destructive power is so vast that our mother is obliged to call us to account. Isn't the population explosion alone not a clear sign of this? Nature itself has limits.

~

Overpopulation, poverty,
and birth control

More than five billion people in the world is too many. Morally, it's a mistake because it aggravates the distortion between rich and poor countries. And on a practical level, it's a disaster. We could ensure that everyone has enough to eat if we mitigated the power of commercial interests, which is not so simple to do. But it is far less certain that we could ensure that everyone has enough to drink.

~

Population growth is related to poverty, and in turn poverty plunders the earth. When people are dying of hunger, they eat everything – grass, insects, everything. They cut down the trees and leave the land dry and bare. All other concerns vanish. That's why in the next 30 years environmental problems will be the hardest that humanity has to face.

I am in favor of birth control. Birth control methods should be publicized and promoted. Forbidding this on ancient religious grounds is definitely harmful sometimes. But how can we make rules more flexible? It is quite normal that

~

the Pope should be directly influenced by the religious traditions he represents. Thus, he is attached to the principle that human life is precious and the maximum number of beings should benefit from it. But there is another principle which contradicts this. It involves a different kind of respect for life: the wish to protect all life, not only human life but also the lives of animals and all living beings. These two principles are in conflict.

For Buddhists, no choices are ever absolutely right. It seems to me that our intelligence is there so we can use it to be flexible and adaptable. An intelligence that is blocked is not intelligent.

~

If I have to cut off a finger to save the other nine, I would not hesitate – I would cut it off. It's time to break down these barriers. Over five billion precious lives are jostling for space on our planet at the moment, and if we wish to offer them a little more prosperity, justice, and happiness, shouldn't we stop ourselves from multiplying too much? Isn't that logical?

~

The urgency of educating people in the
Third World

The real problem of the Third World is ignorance. Together with attachment and aversion, ignorance is one of the three poisons of the mind, which are the source of all mental suffering. In the Third World, ignorance is certainly the most serious of the three. In the West, you are beginning to realize that something is wrong, and in your own way you are organizing yourselves and battling against it.

So we must educate the people of the Third World because they have very little understanding. And this must be done in a dynamic way, without any sentimental shyness. The need is immediate and urgent. We must communicate clearly to dispel misunderstanding: "You are heading in the wrong direction. Your population is growing too fast, and this will lead to even greater hardship. It is natural that you want your living standards to rise. But this cannot happen for everyone. On the contrary."

~

The suffering of animals

We can see how animals suffer. We can see how people abuse them, hit them, and use them cruelly in medical experiments. We can see how we exploit them as draught animals, and how they are sacrificed for their meat. We should develop kindness to animals. We should take account of their suffering, and consider that maybe one day we might be reborn as an animal ourselves.

Thousands of animals, or rather millions and billions of animals, are slaughtered for food. This is distressing. But my sadness reaches its height

~

when I think of intensive rearing methods. In these cases, the poor animals undergo a veritable hell. From the Buddhist point of view, all living beings – that is, beings with feelings, experiences, and sensations – are considered equal. Human beings can live without eating meat. As human beings, I think that deep down our nature tends towards vegetarianism and leads us to do everything in our power to prevent harming other species.

~

The only true guardian of peace

In modern society, despite sophisticated policing systems with advanced technology, acts of terrorism still take place. Although one side has many sophisticated techniques for keeping track of the other side, that other side is becoming more creative in carrying out their crimes. The only true guardian of peace lies within: a sense of concern and responsibility for your own future and an altruistic concern for the wellbeing of others.

~

Western civilization

Western civilization is very advanced on the material level. If it were as fertile in developing techniques for inner development as it is in developing technology, it would be at the forefront of the modern world. But when man forgets to cultivate his inner life, he turns himself into a machine and becomes a slave to material things. Then he is a human being only in name.

~

The Western technological mirage

Right now, all of the Eastern nations are trying to copy Western technology. We Easterners, and Tibetans like myself, look to Western technology feeling that once we develop material progress our people will reach some permanent state of happiness. But when I come to Europe or North America, I see that underneath the beautiful surface there is still unhappiness, frustration, and restlessness. This shows that material progress alone does not provide a complete answer for human beings.

~

Technology is amazing because it produces results, and often immediate results. Unlike prayer! There is nothing wrong with technology per se, or with material progress. But is the human mind able to adapt to this technology, to feel comfortable with it, and not get intoxicated by it?

~

A new social model

We must attempt the impossible. I am convinced that if we continue to follow a social model that is entirely conditioned by money and power, and that takes so little account of true values such as love and altruism, future generations may have to face far worse problems and endure even more terrible forms of suffering.

I have been told that young people in the United States, and even in Europe, are behaving in increasingly selfish and cruel ways. I have heard that suburbs are like jungles, that there are young

~

gangsters who take drugs, that young people throw stones from bridges causing fatal car accidents, and even that crimes are committed by children. Is this the result of general moral decadence, or of an economic crisis, or is it because seeing violence on television every day incites our own violent streak?

Each one of us lacks one thing or another. I am not exactly sure what we lack, but I can feel we lack something. In the West, even if at the moment you are going through a crisis, you actually have everything, or at least you think you do; all kinds of material goods are there, and are no doubt

~

distributed better than they were in the past. But it seems to me that you are living in a constant state of tension, in an atmosphere of never-ending competitiveness and fear. And those who are brought up in such an atmosphere will find themselves lacking all their lives: they will not know that wonderful quality of depth and intimacy that is the richness of life. They will stay on the surface of the troubled sea, without ever knowing the calm that lies beneath.

~

The death penalty

I am absolutely opposed to the death penalty. My predecessor abolished it in Tibet. Today, I find it hard to believe that it persists in large countries like China and India. In the name of justice, they are still killing people in the country of Mahatma Gandhi. In the very land where the Buddha taught. The death penalty is pure violence, a barbaric and useless violence. Dangerous even, because it can only lead to other acts of violence – as all violence does. The supreme punishment ought to be a life sentence, and without brutality.

~

Karma is our judge

If more people believed in the law of karma, we would never need a police force or peace treaties. But without an inner conviction that nobody can escape the consequences of their actions, even if we employ many types of external means in order to enforce the law, we will never be able to build a peaceful society. Modern societies use very sophisticated equipment to monitor and identify criminals. But the more complicated and fascinating our equipment is, the more sophisticated and determined the criminals become. If human society is to improve, it is not enough to enforce

~

external laws. We need to have recourse to our inner judge.

~

The power and responsibility of the media

Let's consider the situation with the media. On television, for example, every day there is an emphasis on sex and violence. I doubt that the producers of such programs really want to harm society. But their priority is just financial profit, and they don't appear to have any sense of social responsibility. On the other side, the audience seems to like the sensations that these programs produce, so viewers share the blame, too. In a situation like this, where influences converge, what can we do? Each one of us is responsible

~

for reducing the negative potential of every situation we have to face. If we wish to change the world, first we must improve and transform ourselves.

Political and religious leaders should acknowledge that nowadays they are not the only ones who wield power and authority. The power of the press is well known and well researched. The power of radio, and especially of television, is now becoming central. The power of the media is a real power which acts on us directly or indirectly, and which modifies our behavior, our tastes, and probably our thinking. Like any authority, it cannot be

~

applied at random. This power gives journalists a responsibility comparable to that of religious and political leaders. In their own way, they too are contributing to the establishment and maintenance of a human community, and the wellbeing of that community should be their first concern.

~

An exalting task for all mankind

The West is fascinated by efficiency. And there is
no doubt that in many areas its efficiency is quite
admirable. That is why I would like to ask this
question, which seems natural to me: why not
apply this technical efficiency to protect *all* forms
of life? This would be an exalting task for all
mankind, especially as we seem to lack a truly
large-scale project or ideal. It is difficult, yet it is
absolutely necessary. If the question of human
survival is not solved, there will be nobody left to
solve the problem. And Buddhism can help here.

~

We stand at the dawn of a new age, where concepts and extremist dogmas no longer dominate human affairs. We should use this historical opportunity to replace them with spiritual and human values, and to ensure that these values become the very fabric of the great human family that is beginning to emerge.

CHAPTER FOUR

FAITH, SCIENCE, AND RELIGION

~

Religion

One might say that religion is a kind of luxury. If you have a religion, that is good. But it is clear that even without religion we can manage. However, without basic human qualities such as love, compassion, and kindness, we cannot survive. They are essential to our own peace and mental stability.

~

The point of religious diversity

All religions share a common root, which is limitless compassion. They emphasize human improvement, love, respect for others, and compassion for the suffering of others. Insofar as love is essential in every religion, we could say that love is a universal religion. But the various techniques and methods for developing love and attaining salvation or liberation differ widely between the traditions. I don't think there could ever be just one single philosophy or one single religion. Since there are so many different types of people, with a range of tendencies and

~

inclinations, it is quite fitting that there are differences between religions. And the fact that there are so many different descriptions of the religious path shows how rich religion is.

~

Belief, experience, and reason
in Buddhism

Buddhism states that man is his own master, or that he has the potential to become his own master. This is the very basis of Buddhist philosophy and we have developed considerable experience of a great number of different methods in order to reach self mastery. Mind is the creator of our world, in every moment. That is why responsibility is so crucially connected with our mind.

Buddhism has always refrained from asserting the existence and the omnipotence of a creator god.

~

Yet that does not mean that our beliefs are only rational. We acknowledge the existence of higher beings, or at least of a certain higher state of being; we believe in oracles, in premonitions, in dream interpretation, and in rebirth. But we don't attempt to impose these beliefs on anyone else, even though for us they are certainties. We never try to convert. Buddhism is an experience ... and an experience that is personal. One of the main teachings of the Buddha is: "Rely only on yourself."

In general, the emphasis is always firmly placed on analyzing and researching the teachings yourself.

~

We need to be open-minded and explore them, so when we come across a truth or a law we should not accept it as valid merely on account of our obedience to dogma or our faith in the Buddha. In this sense, I feel that the basic approach of Buddhism is quite similar to the scientific approach.

In general, Buddhists accept whatever is acknowledged to be a fact. Now, Buddhists believe in rebirth. But let's imagine that thanks to various types of research, science one day came to a definitive conclusion that rebirth does not exist; then, if that were utterly proven we would have

~

to accept it, and we would accept it. Basically, the Buddhist attitude on any subject is one that is in accord with the known facts.

~

Who was the Buddha?

Buddha Shakyamuni, or *Gautama Buddha*, was born in India in a royal family of the Shakya clan, over 2,500 years ago. He lived the first part of his life as a prince, but then, having witnessed suffering, he became aware of just how fragile human life is. As a result, he renounced his kingdom in order to dedicate himself to the life of an ascetic.

From the human point of view, his life was marked by 12 "deeds" or events: his descent from Tushita heaven, his conception, his birth, his studies, his marriage, his renunciation, his fasting, his meditation at the foot of the Bodhi tree, his victory over *Mara* (the forces of ignorance), his attainment of enlightenment, his ministry, and his liberation from *samsara*. When he undertook the path, the Buddha accepted all kinds of hardships, sacrificing his body, his loved ones, and his possessions in order to dedicate himself to hearing and practicing the teachings.

The Buddha attained total purification of his mind, speech, and body. We consider that before his enlightenment he was a man like any other. It was through his own efforts that he

~

became the Buddha. And after reaching complete enlightenment, he gave an enormous number of teachings responding to our many interests and concerns, with the aim of liberating all living beings from suffering. His ministry spanned 45 years. He taught the path of cause and effect, on which certain things are to be adopted and others abandoned. He also taught that our future is in our own hands, not in the hands of God nor in the hands of the Buddha.

~

I am not trying to convert anyone

For certain people, Buddhism may simply not be an answer. Different religions meet different people's needs. I do not try to convert people to Buddhism. What I try to explore is how we Buddhists can make a contribution to human society in accordance with our ideas and values.

~

The Buddha's message for
these troubled times

The Buddha taught that life is our most precious asset, and that we should consider that the lives of others are even more precious and important than our own. Some ideologies become less relevant with the passage of time, but this message and teaching is still just as relevant today. In fact in these modern times, when the total destruction of the world is a real threat, the Buddha's message appears to be more convincing than ever.

~

The Buddha and Christ

Just as the Buddha was an example of tolerance and contentment, Christ too dedicated his life to the service of others in a completely disinterested way. Most great teachers have lived saintly lives, preferring the simple life of ordinary folk to the luxury of royal or imperial courts. Their inner strength was prodigious, and their inspiration immeasurable. Externally, they were content with very little and lived simply. One has to conclude that material benefits alone cannot fulfill human aspirations.

~

Our goal

What is our goal? Actually, Buddhists should save all beings. Even if we can't expand our thinking so as to include beings living in other worlds, we ought to take all human beings on this planet into consideration, and in this way we have a practical starting point.

When we practice initially, as a basis we control ourselves, refraining as much as we can from bad actions that hurt others. This is defensive. After that, as we develop certain qualities, then our goal is to help others proactively and effectively, not

~

only in our prayers but also in our daily lives. It is on the basis of this sort of attitude that world peace can develop in a real and lasting way, as well as harmony between individuals.

~

What it means to be a Buddhist

Buddhists differ from non-Buddhists in two respects: in terms of their practice they take refuge in the *Three Jewels*; and in terms of their beliefs they accept the Four Seals characterizing any doctrine as Buddhist. The Three Jewels are the Buddha, the Dharma (his teachings), and the *Sangha*, or community of practitioners. The Four Seals are the four fundamental tenets of Buddhism: all composite phenomena are impermanent; all conditioned phenomena are by nature unsatisfactory; all phenomena are empty of self-existence; and nirvana is true peace.

~

The Buddhist teaching

Usually, when I describe the essence of Buddhism, I say that at best we should try to help others, and if we cannot help them at least we should do them no harm. This teaching grows from the soil of love and compassion.

~

The need for morality

The Buddha himself emphasized the importance of moral discipline. On his deathbed, when he was asked who should succeed him, he replied that morality is the guide and teacher for all Buddhist practitioners. So he effectively named moral discipline as his successor.

Morality is a frame of mind in which we refrain from placing ourselves in any situation that could be harmful to others. Ethical conduct is perfected when we have accomplished the supreme development of the idea of non-harming. In this sense,

~

ethics can be categorized into 10 aspects, each defined as refraining from one of the 10 negative actions. Ethical conduct is like a refreshing shower that extinguishes the fires of attachment, anger, and hatred burning inside us.

~

The 10 negative actions and their four antidotes

There are three doors through which we carry out our actions: the body, speech, and mind. It is through them that we can commit the 10 negative actions. Of these, three relate to the body: killing, stealing, and sexual misconduct. Four relate to speech: lying, divisive speech, harsh speech, and senseless speech or gossip. And finally, three relate to the mind: covetousness, harmful intent, and wrong, or perverse, views. By refraining from these negative actions, and by making a decision not to engage in them, we cultivate positive actions.

~

Even though we might make a serious effort not to commit negative actions, the fact that we have been under the power of delusion for so long sometimes leads us to commit them unconsciously. But we cannot leave our actions there. It is best to undertake the purification practices recommended by the Buddha himself. According to the Buddha, by applying the four antidotes we will be able to purify any negativity already committed. The four antidotes are the power of regret, the power of purification, the power of resolve, and the supreme power of meditation.

~

Why meditate?

It is a great advantage to be able to face life with a positive and balanced spirit. If you train in the long jump, for example, your performance will depend on your physical condition. Your body obeys the laws of matter, which in turn will impose certain constraints on your flexibility. But the mind is simply clarity and awareness. Not only is it free of any limitations of this kind, but with gradual training all its qualities will blossom. Even if you only spend a brief time each day on your meditation practice, you will find it very nourishing. Your mind will lose the habit of being scattered.

~

What can we learn from Buddhism?

It is possible to learn all kinds of lessons from Buddhism without having to follow it completely. For example, one can learn tolerance, without which life is unbearable, and the path leading to peace of mind, which is indispensable for action to be just. This peace of mind is central to what we are looking for in life. It determines the attitude we have towards the world, and towards our neighbors and our enemies too.

The main method to reach it is meditation, which lies at the heart of our practice and our teachings.

~

One of the things that meditation shows us is that the sense of peace already exists within us. We all have a deep desire for it even if it is often hidden, masked, thwarted. Aggression, too, is an intimate part of ourselves. That is precisely why there is a struggle. But our true nature is peaceful. That is why Buddha Shakyamuni advises us to search deeply within, because that is how we will finally satisfy our craving for peace.

~

The path to wisdom

In the profound darkness that we call "fundamental ignorance" lies the root of suffering. Overcoming delusion, our fundamental ignorance, is a lifetime's task. If we are able to engage in sustained practice, then month on month and year on year we will notice a transformation of our mind. However, if we expect realization to happen immediately, or if we expect to gain instant control of our thoughts and emotions, then we will only be disappointed. One of the greatest Tibetan masters, Milarepa, a 12th-century yogi, lived for years like a wild animal and endured numerous hardships in order to attain the highest realization.

~

An inner struggle

In a sense a religious practitioner, whether man or woman, is like a soldier engaged in combat. Who is the enemy? Ignorance, anger, attachment, and pride are the ultimate enemies; they are not outside, but within, and must be fought with the weapons of wisdom and meditative concentration.

We are like a vase designed to
hold knowledge

Listening to the teachings or reading them, we are like a vase designed to hold knowledge. If the vase is placed upside down, even if the gods rained down nectar upon us, it would only trickle away along the outside of the vase. And if the vase is dirty, the nectar would be spoiled. Or again, if the vase has holes in the bottom, the nectar would leak away.

In the same way, if we are easily distracted, we resemble a vase placed upside down. If our attitude

~

is dominated by negative thoughts (such as trying to prove that we are more intelligent or superior), then we are like a dirty container. And finally, if we do not take the teachings to heart, we are like a vase with holes in the bottom.

*Purely theoretical knowledge
is a dangerous thing*

There is a Tibetan story about a pilgrim who was walking around a temple one day, when he came across a man sitting in meditation. He asked him what he was doing, and the meditator replied, "I am practicing patience." On hearing this, the pilgrim hurled insults at him, and immediately the other man became angry. His reaction showed that his practice of patience was only theoretical.

If we had to choose between practical application and theoretical knowledge, practice might be more important than knowledge because whoever has that skill is able to derive full benefit from it. In someone whose mind is not disciplined, knowledge that is purely theoretical can induce and nurture unfortunate states of mind that bring about unpleasantness for oneself and others, instead of the peace of mind that we seek. One might become jealous of those who are higher than oneself, or very competitive towards one's equals, or again arrogant and contemptuous towards inferiors, and so on. It is as though a remedy had turned to poison. It is because this danger is very real that it is always important to link theoretical knowledge with its practical application, and with kindness.

~

Primacy of the teaching over the
teacher

Did not the Buddha, the very embodiment of a teacher, say:

> *"O monks and wise men,*
> *Just as a goldsmith would test his gold*
> *By burning, cutting, and rubbing it,*
> *So must you examine my words and accept them.*
> *But not merely out of reverence for me."*

It is also said: "Rely on the teaching, not on the teacher." This means that we should not judge the validity of a teaching on the basis of a teacher's renown. On the contrary, the proof of whether a master is authentic or not depends on how convincing or implausible his or her teachings are after analysis.

~

The spiritual teacher

It is possible to develop a powerful conviction in the teaching by reading texts on the development of compassion, for example, but when you meet a live person who practices this and who can teach it to you in living situations, your inspiration is all the stronger. The highest realization cannot be achieved without the guidance of an authentic spiritual master.

In the Buddhist tradition, one is a teacher from the point of view of a disciple. There is no other form of certification, like a diploma, that confers on someone the quality of being a spiritual master. You are a lama once you have disciples, it is that simple. The spiritual teacher is responsible for his or her improper behavior. If he abuses his power or displays inappropriate behavior, it is the student's responsibility not to be drawn into it. So the fault belongs to both parties. Partly it is because the student is too obedient and devoted to the spiritual master, having a kind of blind acceptance of that person's guidance. This always spoils the teacher. But of course part of the blame lies with the spiritual master, because he lacks the integrity that is necessary to be immune to that kind of vulnerability.

~

The teacher-student relationship

When you cultivate a relationship with a spiritual teacher, it is important not to take him or her too hastily as your spiritual master. The student-teacher relationship is exceptionally intense. So it is better to consider him or her as a spiritual companion or spiritual friend for as long as necessary – for up to two years, five years, or 10 years at most. During this period, you observe his behavior closely, and take note of his attitudes and his way of teaching, until you are certain of his integrity. At that point, there is no need for a certificate. But it is crucial to begin with a circumspect and resolute approach.

~

The great Tibetan scholar Sakya Pandita (1182–1251) used to say that we usually take great care of worldly matters, like choosing the best horses, so when we decide to practice Dharma, it is important to be even more selective about the practices and the master we follow, because the goal here is more than the means of transport itself.

~

The bodhisattva

For us, a *bodhisattva* is the ideal being. He or she is able to reach nirvana, the state of absolute rest in clear light, but refuses to abide in that state and prefers to remain in touch with the world of suffering beings in order to help them. In other words, he or she will not be able to taste true rest as long as the slightest trace of suffering remains in the world. We need to produce this *bodhisattva* in ourselves. If I say with conviction that my task is to serve all beings, for an indeterminate period, maybe even for a period without end, and that to achieve this goal I will renounce the state of bliss,

~

this requires full and complete determination. Without a strong sense of self, such determination would be impossible.

It is my profound belief that the idea of a *bodhisattva* is better adapted to today's world than many other religious ideas. The experience of a *bodhisattva*, this power of compassion that we discover constantly abiding within our otherwise inconstant nature, is no doubt one of the main factors that is attracting more and more interest in Buddhism.

~

The practice of a bodhisattva

The entire practice of a *bodhisattva* is divided into *six perfections*, which are generosity, discipline, patience, effort, meditative concentration, and wisdom. In order to fulfill the hopes of others, it is very important to engage in the practice of generosity, which in turn should be strengthened by a strict observance of ethical discipline, that is, of non-violence. The practice of discipline must itself be complemented by that of patience, because you will need to have forbearance when facing the harm inflicted on you by others. In order to succeed in these practices, your endeavor must

~

be strong and stable. And without meditative concentration that effort will not be so effective. Finally, if you do not have the wisdom that realizes the nature of all phenomena, you will not be capable of guiding others on the path that leads to enlightenment.

~

The sweet taste of bodhicitta

If there is one practice that is sufficient to bring about buddhahood, it is the practice of great compassion. Chandragomin, a sixth-century Indian poet, said that it is stupid to expect to change the taste of a very bitter fruit by simply adding one or two drops of sugar to it. In the same way, we cannot expect the fragrance of our minds, which are so contaminated by the bitter taste of delusion, to change instantaneously into the sweet taste of *bodhicitta* or compassion on the basis of just one or two sessions of meditation. Sustained and continuous effort is extremely important.

As the Buddha himself said, on the strength of their wisdom *bodhisattvas* abandon all delusion, but through the vigor of applying compassionate methods, they never abandon beings.

~

The powers of a buddha

A buddha has the ability to perceive the personal capacity of every being according to whether it is supreme, average, or weak. He has the power to know the past lives of others, as well as when they will die and how they will be reborn, according to their *karma*. A buddha's mind is also omniscient. It can apprehend the entire sphere of phenomena without exception because it has reached a state that is totally free of obstructions to knowledge.

The mind of a buddha is never separate from the essence of reality. There are no thoughts in a buddha's mind. Nothing suggests to him that he should help beings, but by virtue of his great compassion he plants the root of wellbeing in people's hearts, and they draw strength from this both for their worldly life and their spiritual benefit.

The body, speech, and mind of the buddhas act tirelessly for the benefit of others. They fulfill the aspirations of living beings and lead them, step by step, with the appropriate skill and in accordance with their diverse needs, dispositions, and interests. As soon as they see beings suffer, the minds of the buddhas are spontaneously activated

～

by a limitless compassion that has the potential
of increasing to infinity.

~

The buddha seed

We should never forget that even in the most perverted and cruel of human beings exists a seed of love and compassion which will one day cause him or her to become a buddha.

CHAPTER FIVE

THE INNER JOURNEY

~

Peace of mind

Every day I experience the benefits of having peace of mind. It is very good for the body. As you might imagine, I am quite a busy man with many responsibilities, deciding on policies, traveling, and making speeches. All of this is certainly a considerable burden, and yet my blood pressure is that of a baby. Whatever is good for me is also good for others; I have no doubt about that. A good diet, refraining from excessive desires, and daily meditation all lead to peace of mind, and this peace of mind is physically beneficial. Despite all the difficulties we encounter in life, and I have

~

not been spared on that account, we can all experience the effects of such a way of life.

~

The questions we should ask
ourselves

"Who am I?", "What is the nature of my mind?", "What advantage is there in cultivating kind thoughts?", "What can we gain from harmful thoughts?" Never stop asking yourself these questions. Reflecting on these points will show you just how much of a spoilsport your mind is, and how necessary it is to tame it.

~

We all have the same potential

Every human being has the same potential. Whatever makes you feel "I am worthless" is wrong. Absolutely wrong. You are deceiving yourself. We all have the power of thought, so what could you possibly be lacking? If you have the willpower, then you can do anything.

Yet although we all start off with the same capacities, some people develop them and others do not. We get easily used to being mentally lazy, all the more easily because laziness hides beneath the appearance of activity: we run right and left,

~

we make calculations, phone calls, and so on. But these activities engage only the most elementary and coarse levels of the mind. They hide the essential from us.

~

Love and compassion are
fundamental

What brings about happiness? Happiness is related to the way we think. If we do not train our minds, and do not reflect on life, it is impossible to find happiness.

The qualities of love and compassion are utterly fundamental. I consider compassion to be the basis and supreme support of humankind. This eminent quality that induces us to love our neighbor, to come to his aid when he is suffering, and to forget ourselves for his sake, is one that only

~

human beings are capable of awakening. And whenever they do so, they are the first to derive happiness from it.

~

By nature we are social animals

Insofar as we are social animals, human beings are not capable of living in isolation. If we were solitary by nature, there would be no towns and villages. On the contrary, nature requires us to live cooperatively in society. Those of us who do not have a sense of responsibility, or who do not believe in the common good, act against human nature. In order to ensure the survival of the human race, we need authentic cooperation mainly based on a sense of brotherhood and sisterhood. In fact, as human beings and social animals, it is quite natural for us to love others.

~

Without the love of our parents at the dawn of our life, what would have become of us? And when we grow old, we will once again depend on the kindness of others. In both cases, we are at the mercy of others. But between childhood and old age we live a period of relative independence, and since at that time we are able to do without others, we think it is unnecessary to be kind towards them.

~

Love based on attachment

Love based on attachment is limited and precarious. It mainly involves projection. Imagine, for example, that a very attractive person appears and you are immediately drawn to them. Today you are in love, but tomorrow it is quite possible that your feelings will turn hostile. Love based on attachment is of no real help. What does it bring us, if not irritation and annoyance? We believe that true compassion is free of attachment. This compassion is expressed spontaneously and unconditionally, like that of a mother who expects nothing from her child in return. It is such a demanding form

~

of love that it gives birth to an indomitable desire
to make all beings happy. It strives ceaselessly to
ensure that everyone is free of suffering and of
everything that brings about suffering.

~

Happiness and anxiety

The main reason that people inflict suffering on others is that they do not understand the true nature of happiness. They think that others' pain will in some way bring about their own happiness, or that their own happiness is more important than that of others, regardless of any suffering incurred in the process of securing it. In the long run, causing others to suffer and trampling on their rights to a peaceful and happy existence only lead to one's own anxiety, fear, and doubt.

～

Like ripples on a lake

Worldly activities are like ripples on a lake: hardly has one disappeared than another one emerges. It is endless. Worldly activity will never stop until death. Now that we have obtained a precious human life, it would be such a pity if we were not to open ourselves up a little to the influence of Dharma. We should seize every opportunity to practice the truth and to improve ourselves, instead of waiting for a time when we are less busy.

~

Enemies are precious

Enemies are precious in the sense that they help us to grow. If I had stayed in Lhasa, and if the Chinese invasion had never taken place, I might still be very isolated. I would probably be more conservative than I am now.

When, at some point in our lives, we meet a real tragedy, we can react in one of two ways. Obviously, we can lose hope and let ourselves slip into despair, into alcohol, drugs, and unending sadness. Or else we can wake ourselves up, discover in ourselves an energy that was hidden there, and act with greater clarity and more force.

~

Anyone who feels overwhelmed
has no power over reality

I am a simple Buddhist monk, and although my experience is in no way exceptional, I have been able to taste the benefits of developing an attitude of love, compassion, and respect for all human beings. For many years I have been trying to cultivate these qualities and, despite difficult circumstances, I realize that this approach has made me a happy man. Anyone who feels overwhelmed has no power over reality. Knowing how to accept the blows dealt by fate means never giving up.

~

Karma

Pleasure and pain come from your own past actions. So it is easy to define *karma* in one short sentence: "Act well, and things will go well; act wrongly, and things will go wrong."

~

The four powers of regret,
purification, resolve, and meditation

There are four antidotes against negative actions: the power of regret, the power of purification, the power of resolve, and the supreme power of meditation. Although using the appropriate antidotes enables us to purify negative actions completely, and to destroy their potential for bringing about unfavorable consequences in the future, it is much better by far not to commit any negative actions in the first place. It's a bit like when one breaks a leg: it always heals, but compared to a leg that has never been broken it is far more fragile.

~

Responsibility for ourselves

When the Buddha teaches that we are our own master, that everything depends on us, he is indicating that pleasure and displeasure come from virtuous and non-virtuous acts respectively, that they are forged not externally but deep within ourselves. The Buddhist theory about the responsibility we have for ourselves is particularly relevant. It invites us to question ourselves, and to tame ourselves in our own interest and that of others.

~

Aggression

There are so many circumstances that make us unjust, ambitious, or aggressive. All around us, everything is pushing us in that direction, often out of some commercial interest: "I have to possess this or that object, otherwise I will be miserable. In order to have it I will have to earn extra money. And in order to earn this extra money, I will have to fight and compete against others." That is how your aggression will come up again.

~

Cruelty

To be cruel is tantamount to stopping in the middle of the path. It is like renouncing the attempt to go deeply inside ourselves. It is being attached to the surface reality, and becoming irritated or exasperated by it. And yet harmony does exist. We have all experienced it at times. It resides in the depths of our being. It is our primordial nature.

~

Kindness

Having a heart, and a kind and warm disposition, is an enormous advantage. Not only does it bring us joy, but we can share this joy with others. Relations between individuals, nations, and continents deteriorate only from lack of goodwill and kindness, even though these qualities are so valuable and necessary for the quality of life in society. That is why it is worth trying to develop them.

~

Slander

It is more useful to be aware of a single weakness in oneself than to be aware of a thousand weaknesses in someone else. Rather than speaking badly of other people, or talking in a way that provokes conflict or problems in their lives, we should adopt a purer attitude towards them.

~

Anger

If your mind is dominated by anger, you will lose the greatest part of your human intelligence: wisdom, that is the ability to discern between good and evil. Anger is one of the greatest problems that we have to face in the world today.

In the course of our daily human relations, if we speak straightforwardly and in a reasoned way, anger is not necessary. Any points of difference can be discussed. Whenever we cannot justify ourselves through reason, that is when anger rises. It is when reason ends that anger begins. In my

~

experience, even if anger gives us the strength to react or to respond in the event of conflict, the energy it gives us is blind and difficult to control. The only advantage that anger has is the energy it brings us, but we could find this energy just as well from other sources without having to harm ourselves or others. Anger is a sign of weakness.

~

Complacency

The image we have of ourselves tends to be complacent. We look at ourselves with indulgence. Whenever something unpleasant happens to us, we always have the tendency to cast the blame on others, or on fate, a demon, or a god. We shrink from looking into ourselves, as the Buddha recommended.

~

The human mind

Owing to our lack of control and our weaknesses, our ordinary minds are not able to understand the nature of reality. And yet this is the most essential thing to do if we want to free ourselves or others from the cycle of birth and death. So we must shape our minds into an instrument that is able to discern reality, rather like a microscope. We have to turn our minds into an effective weapon to cut the root of suffering, so it becomes as sharp as the blade of a sword.

~

Ourselves and others

If we love both ourselves and other people, then both we and they will experience moments of happiness. But when we love ourselves more than our fellows, we create various types of suffering not only for ourselves but also for them. Even though you are equal to others in terms of your right to happiness and to the absence of suffering, nevertheless this notion of equality implies that you are just one single person whereas your fellow human beings are countless. We should therefore reflect on the mistake we make by loving ourselves first and foremost.

~

Using visualization to increase
compassion

Visualization is a very efficient method for increasing compassion.

First, visualize yourself as an impartial person in the middle. Then to your right, visualize someone who seeks only their own wellbeing, thinking only of himself, seizing every opportunity to reach his goal ... and yet who is constantly dissatisfied. To your left, visualize a group of people who are obviously experiencing suffering and who are asking for help. As the reasonable hope of all human

~

beings is to find happiness and avoid suffering, everyone has equal rights. Now reflect on this; objectively. Wisely. The neutral and impartial person in the middle will hardly feel the urge to join the selfish miser to his right. As for you, if you are generous, you will naturally wish to join the group to the left. And the closer you get to the group, the more your selfishness will evaporate, and the more your altruism will grow.

Practicing this visualization on a daily basis is a constant help.

~

Three ways of relating

Usually we classify people into one of three categories: friends, enemies, and strangers. On meeting them, we adopt three types of attitude: desire, aversion, and indifference. As long as these three modes of relating are predominant, it is impossible to give birth to an altruistic frame of mind. It is therefore important to neutralize attachment, hostility, and indifference.

~

A prison unto ourselves

The tyrants that dominate us and bind us to them at the same time are desire and hatred. They manifest as soon as we enter the terribly solid, dark, and impregnable prison of grasping at our self and what is ours as though they were real. What leads us astray is the "thick darkness" of our wrong view, which holds that all phenomena, and especially ourselves, have inherent existence. This is why we are tossed about by the four violent currents of the river of suffering: birth, old age, illness, and death.

~

The imaginary "I"

There is an enormous difference between the way things appear and the way they are in reality. The fact that we cannot prove that objects exist when we analyze them shows that they do not exist in and of themselves. If things did have an intrinsic existence, then they would not be mutually dependent on each other. Asserting that the existence of objects depends on the consciousness of the subject that names them is tantamount to saying that they only exist insofar as they are labeled. You can try this out for yourself. Observe what you call "I." The context in which it appears is that of

~

the body and mind. And yet if you analyze these two supports of the "I," you cannot find any "I" there. All that is left after analysis is the simple "I" that exists by dint of our imagination and conceptualization.

~

Being wisely selfish

Even if your selfishness is a fact, then let it be a wise selfishness free of narrow-mindedness, and free of thinking of everything in terms of yourself. Who is refusing happiness? Who stubbornly holds on to stupidity? Who is content with frustration? If you want to be selfish, then let your selfishness be well informed rather than irrational.

There are two sorts of ego. One corresponds to a very high idea we have of ourselves. This type of ego is extreme, it is a false path and only brings trouble. The other corresponds to a strong feeling

~

we have that "I can do it," "I should do it," "I should take on this responsibility." This sense of self is necessary. It is the basis of human determination and courage. If we lose this it provokes discouragement, self-doubt, and self-hatred.

~

The positive and negative aspects of ego

Desires can be either negative or positive. If I desire to acquire something for myself – let's say I desire good health when I am ill, or a bowl of rice when I am hungry – such a desire is perfectly justified. The same applies to selfishness, which can be either negative or positive.

In most cases, asserting oneself only leads to disappointment, or to conflict with other egos that feel as exclusively about their existence as we do about our own. This is especially true when a strongly developed ego indulges in capricious or demanding behavior. The illusion of having a permanent self is a secret danger that stalks us all: "I want this," "I want that." It can even lead us to kill. Excessive selfishness leads to uncontrollable perversions, which always end badly. But on the other hand, a firm confident sense of self can be a very positive element. Without a strong sense of self, that is, of one's skills, potential, and convictions, nobody can take on significant responsibilities. Responsibility requires true self-confidence. How could a mother without hands save her child from the river?

~

Our happiness comes from others

In this world, all qualities spring from preferring the wellbeing of others to our own, whereas frustrations, confusion, and pain result from selfish attitudes. By adopting an altruistic outlook and by treating others in the way they deserve, our own happiness is assured as a byproduct. We should realize that self-centeredness is the source of all suffering, and that thinking of others is the source of all happiness.

~

Education

I am totally convinced that the best source of happiness and peace for a human being is compassion and love. Anger and hatred tend to bring about only mental confusion and agitation. From this point of view, I think education is very important. I have been very moved to find that the way we look after children in their earliest years has a big impact on the rest of their lives. On the one hand, a child needs adequate food, but on the other hand, without the tender care and affection of its parents, it will not reach full maturation. This has been shown through scientific research. So the

~

importance and effectiveness of having a loving attitude towards others has been scientifically established. Some people may think to themselves, "What rubbish! I can make my way very well in life without having the slightest sense of responsibility." However, it is quite evident that this is not the case.

~

Confidence breeds success

If you wish to succeed in whatever you are doing, it is necessary to have confidence, in other words to develop courage. Your confidence should be such that you should be prepared to undertake each task by yourself, without depending on the collaboration or the help of others. Nobody has ever achieved anything without confidence. By developing courage, and by making the necessary effort, even things that previously seemed complicated and difficult turn out to be simple and easy.

~

Defeat and victory

If someone treats you badly, abuses you, or even strikes you physically out of jealousy or dislike, rather than responding in kind you should suffer the defeat yourself and allow the other person to have the victory. If circumstances are such that there is no great benefit to be gained through taking a small loss, then you can, without any hatred but with a motivation of compassion, respond in a strong manner.

~

True friends and false

Friendship can be viewed in various ways. Sometimes, we might think that we have to have money and power in order to have friends, but that is not true. As long as our fortune is intact, such friends will appear to be loyal, but they will abandon us as soon as our prosperity starts to diminish. These are not true friends, they are just friends of money and power. Genuine friendship is based on true human feeling, a feeling of closeness in which there is a sense of sharing and connectedness. The factor that sustains that friendship is whether or not the two people have mutual feelings of love

~

and affection. Everyone needs friends, and it's quite simple: compassion and concern for others are what attract friends.

~

Sexual desire

Sexual desire, by definition, wants satisfaction by the possession of another person. To a large extent this is a mental projection, stimulated by a certain emotion. We imagine the other in our possession. In that moment of desire, everything seems agreeable and desirable. One sees no obstacle to it, no reason for restraint. The desired object seems to have no defects, and to be utterly worthy of praise. Once the desire subsides – whether it considers itself satisfied, or it weakens with time – we no longer view the other person in the same way. Some people admit they are stunned by this. Each

~

one discovers the true nature of the other. That is why there are so many broken marriages, quarrels, lawsuits, and so much hatred.

~

Limiting one's desires

Even if you had the world at your feet, it would still not be enough. Desire is insatiable. And on top of that, how many obstacles there are in the endless searching, how many disappointments and difficulties, and how much suffering! Excessive desire is not only impossible to satisfy, it's also the source of torment. Let's imagine that you are extraordinarily rich, and you have a huge stock of food. But you have only one mouth and one stomach, so you cannot swallow more than an ordinary person. If you ate enough for two, you would die. It's better to establish boundaries right from the start, and feel satisfied within those boundaries.

~

Giving

It's best not to be possessive about your belongings, nor to busy yourself trying to store more and
more things, because possessions are an obstacle to
the practice of generosity, which is one of the *six
perfections*. If you feel incapable of separating
yourself from something, you should reflect on the
futility of material goods, as well as the impermanence of your own life. Sooner or later, you will
have to leave your possessions behind, so rather
than dying in the grip of avarice it is wiser to free
yourself from them and donate them right away.
Whoever realizes how futile it is to feel possessive,

~

and who is generous to others with the pure hope
of helping them, is called a *bodhisattva*.

~

Effort and diligence

It is said that effort should be like a river, sustained and continuous. If you have the gift of perfect effort or diligence, free of any sense of discouragement or inadequacy, then everything you do will succeed. Effort is said to be the precondition for all positive actions. It protects you against discouragement and depression in the event of difficulties. Your diligence should be so unshakable that even if you had to be reborn in hell for thousands of years in order to fulfill the wishes of a single individual, you would be prepared to do that.

~

Other people

Since beginningless time, in the course of rebirths which must be infinite in number, every being has been included within your sphere of existence, and has established a relationship with you just like the one you enjoy with your mother in this life. You must make this your strong conviction. And on the basis of this understanding, you will gradually begin to consider all beings as friends.

~

Anger and judgment

Sometimes we have to endure harm inflicted by others, and anger and hatred destroy our capacity for judgment, so instead of returning their kindness we act in retaliation. By losing self-control, and by giving an eye for an eye in return for every tiny experience of suffering that I feel incapable of bearing, I will accumulate negative actions that will have an effect in the long term. When someone hits us, our pain is due just as much to the inside workings of our body as to the wound itself. In fact if we had no body, we would not experience physical pain. So if we want to get angry about it, we should also be angry at our own body.

~

Treating other people
as you would a treasure

Beware of feeling indifferent to other people. Treat them with the respect you would a treasure that has the power to enable you to achieve your worldly and ultimate goals. Make each person the sole object of your love. Let others be more dear to you, and more precious, than you consider yourself, because from the very first step on the path to liberation you will need them in order to cultivate your altruistic aspiration to reach supreme enlightenment.

~

Joy

We should also cultivate the power of joy. When one engages in the practice of the *six perfections*, it is very important that they be carried out with a sense of joy. One's joyful enthusiasm should be similar to the motivation and attitude of a child that is fully absorbed in sports or play.

~

Marriage

On the subject of love and marriage, my simple opinion is that making love is alright, but for marriage, don't hurry, be cautious. Make sure you will remain together forever, or at least for this whole life. If you do, then your union can be a happy one. A happy home is one step towards a happy world.

~

The mind is primordially pure

If we disturb the water of a lake it will become muddy, but the nature of water itself is not muddied. We only have to let the waters grow calm again for the mud to settle at the bottom, and the water will regain its original purity. What can we do to restore our mind to its original purity? How can we eradicate the various factors in mental pollution? We cannot get rid of them through outside struggles, nor by ignoring them, but only by injecting powerful antidotes via the channel of meditation. If you are able to practice meditation a little every day, gathering your scattered mind by

~

focusing on an internal object, that would be a great help. The stream of thoughts thinking of good things, bad things, and so on, will quieten down. You will find it's like taking a short vacation: finding yourself beyond your thoughts, and resting there.

~

Pride

If you assume a humble attitude, your own good qualities will increase, whereas when you are full of pride there is no way to be happy. You will become jealous of others, angry with them, and look down on them, due to which an unpleasant atmosphere will be created and unhappiness in society will increase.

~

Drop the past

If a misfortune has already occurred, it is best not to worry about it, so we do not add fuel to the problem. Don't ally yourself with past events by lingering on them and exaggerating them. Let the past take care of itself, and transport yourself to the present while taking whatever measures are necessary to ensure that such a misfortune never occurs again, now or in the future.

~

Purity

It is said that buddhahood should not be sought anywhere but within one's own mind, for the elements that are needed to realize it reside in us. Deep inside us, the pure seed and essence of buddhahood, the *tathagatagarbha*, awaits its full blossoming into buddhahood.

~

Respect

Courtesy, tact, and diplomacy are no doubt excellent qualities, but they are superficial ones. Whereas having a mind that is open, direct, and genuine enables us to go much more deeply into our relationships. The qualities of the heart are essential for good communication. Nowadays, relations have been rather dehumanized. This has led to a lack of respect for our fellow men, and we end up thinking of them as no more than cogs in a machine.

~

Taking the reins is the key to happiness

The state of mind of a Buddhist practitioner should be stable, and should not be subject to too many conflicting events. Such a person will feel both joy and pain, but neither will be too weak or too intense. Stability is developed through discipline. The heart and mind become more full of energy, more resolute, and therefore less susceptible to being blown about by outside events.

Deep within the human being abides the wisdom that can support him or her in the face of negative situations. In this way, events no longer throw him

~

because he is holding the reins. Similarly, when something good happens it is also possible to rein it in. Taking the reins is the key to happiness. In Tibet we have a saying: "If you are beside yourself with joy, tears are not far behind." This shows how relative what we call joy and pain are.

~

The virtues of patience

In daily life we experience suffering more often than pleasure. If we are patient, in the sense of taking suffering voluntarily upon ourselves, even if we are not capable of doing this physically, then we will not lose our capacity for judgment. We should remember that if a situation cannot be changed, there is no point in worrying about it. If it can be changed, then there is no need to worry about it either, we should simply go about changing it.

~

The remedy for fear

One of the methods for working on our deepest fears is to consider that they have been produced by our past actions. Then, depending on whether the object of your fear is emotional suffering or physical pain, examine it well and ask yourself whether there is any remedy for it. If there is, why be afraid? If there is nothing you can do, then there is even less point in worrying about it. There is also another approach, which entails looking for the person who is afraid. Look at the nature of your self. Where is it? Who is it that says "I"? What is the nature of this self? You will find this very fruitful.

The middle way

Moderation should be applied even to our daily meals: our stomach would be glad if we adopted moderation, because too much food makes it ill, and too little damages it. We should never fall into excess in either direction: to be too conservative is not good, and to be too radical isn't either. The Buddhist philosophy of "the middle way" is to find the happy medium.

~

Telling the truth

As a general rule, we should tell the truth. However, there are certain cases where this could be disastrous. For instance, when telling the truth could be hurtful, or not bring the slightest benefit, then it is better to remain silent.

Imagine a monk who is approached by hundreds of hunters who ask him whether he has seen an animal pass by. If he has, what should he do? As a monk, he should tell the truth. But in this precise situation, if he is truthful the hunters will find the animal and kill it. So in such a case, it is better to hide the truth.

~

Tolerance

The basis of all moral teaching should be not to retaliate in the event of attack. Of course, compassion and tolerance are just words and words have no power in themselves. Our first inclination is always to retaliate, to react, and even sometimes to take revenge, which only leads to more suffering. This is why Buddhism always says: "Calm your mind." Meditation can help you find tolerance within. When you have practiced it, you will see how it benefits you. And then you can extend that to those around you through example.

～

Being mindful

When a soldier lets go of his sword, he immediately takes hold of it again without hesitation. Similarly, when you make an effort to do something, you should be constantly mindful so you do not fall prey to negative states of mind. Your mindfulness should be that of someone who is forced to walk with a full glass of milk on his head, and who is under sentence of death if a single drop escapes.

~

Dedicating our work to helping others

Helping just one person is still helping. You can be directly useful by working in education and health; or you could work in a large firm or a factory. Wherever you work, you have the opportunity to help others. Maybe you cannot serve society directly, but the fact that your work is salaried does not prevent it from benefiting everyone. Nevertheless, it is better to work with a good motivation, and try to say to yourself: "I am doing this work with the intention of helping others." Of course, if you manufacture bullets then there is a contradiction. Manipulating ammunition with the thought "I am

~

doing this for the benefit of others" would be pure hypocrisy.

~

Engaging in life full time

You should acknowledge that despite everything you have managed to hoard in this life, even billions of dollars, you will not take a single cent away with you at the time of death. Hence the danger of immersing oneself completely in daily activities that are confined to the present life. The point is not to turn one's back on material life, or to look into one's mind all the time thinking only of future lives; but it would be wise to do this part time, investing half your energy in mundane affairs and half in your inner life.

~

*Towards lay spirituality
and secular ethics*

It is my profound belief that together we need to find a new form of spirituality. It should be developed in parallel with the religions, so that all those of goodwill can follow it, whether they are religious or not. One new concept, for example, is that of lay spirituality. We should promote this idea with the help of the scientific community. It could help us establish what we are all looking for – secular ethics. I believe in this deeply, with the view it will lead to a better world.

CHAPTER SIX

LIFE, DEATH, AND REBIRTH

~

Samsara

Samsara is the cycle of existence (birth, life, death, and rebirth) conditioned by *karma*. It is the wheel of suffering that characterizes the phenomenon we call life.

~

Impermanence

In this cycle of existence, over the course of numerous rebirths, and sometimes even within a single lifetime, everything is changing. There are no certainties. Everything that comes together falls apart, anything high ends up low, meetings finish in separation, and life ends in death. Our happiness is continuously flowing away. And all our belongings are subject to change. Nothing that we normally think of as real is actually permanent.

A new birth never shields anyone from death. On the contrary, we are continuously making our way

~

closer to the moment of death, like animals led to the slaughter. In this world everything is subject to impermanence and will ultimately disintegrate. As the Seventh Dalai Lama used to say, "Young people who seem strong and healthy, but who die young, are masters who teach us impermanence. It is just like in the theater, where the actors change their costumes between roles."

~

The principle of past and future lives

The Buddhist scriptures teach that the mind has no beginning, which means that rebirths have no beginning either. Systematic research leads to the conclusion that the mind can in no sense be the substantial cause of matter, nor can matter be that of the mind. The only acceptable theory is that the substantial cause of the mind must be a pre-existing mind. This is how we argue the principle of past and future lives.

Buddhists say that rebirth is a reality. It is a fact. We believe that there is a subtle consciousness

~

which is the source of everything we call the created world. This subtle consciousness abides in each individual from the beginning of time until buddhahood is attained. That is what we call "being." This "being" can take different forms – animal, human, and ultimately buddha.

For centuries, over a vast span of time, and from life to life, this subtle mind seeks buddhahood. Whereas rebirth is choiceless, the idea of reincarnation involves choice. It denotes the power of certain virtuous people to determine their future rebirth, as was the case for Buddha and for many others.

~

When it has attained a certain refinement, which is what we call the subtle consciousness, our mind can no longer die in the ordinary sense of the term. It can incarnate in another body. This is especially the case with *bodhisattvas*. Standing on the very threshold of *nirvana*, they prefer to renounce this in favor of staying in *samsara* where they continue to help us.

~

Renunciation

It is useless to be attached to this life, because even if we live for one hundred years we will have to die one day. Furthermore, we do not know the hour of our death: it could happen any time. And then our life will have to unravel, and however loved or wealthy we are, we will have no choice. What use will our belongings be to us then? In this sense, to die a millionaire is no better than to die a wild animal. This is why we need to develop a profound sense of aversion for this cycle of hardship, as well as profound renunciation. Then we can begin to examine carefully the causes that lead to such misery and frustration.

~

Our instinctive belief in
an independent self

Suffering does not happen without a cause, no more than it is produced by some all-powerful god. It results from our confusion and from the actions we perform motivated by uncontrolled states of mind. The primary cause of all suffering is ignorance, which is a basic misconception of the nature of phenomena coupled with a reflexive apprehension of itself as inherently existing. It leads us to exaggerate the status of things and events, and devises categories that separate self and other. We then see ourselves as the most precious thing

~

in the universe, and treat others as though we were more precious than a buddha. And yet this tendency to grasp has never brought lasting happiness.

~

Mistaking a rope for a snake

Let's take the example of a piece of rope lying in a dark place: you might mistake the rope for a snake. The mistaken idea that the rope is a snake could trigger various reactions in your mind such as fear, and might provoke you into all sorts of actions such as running out of the house in panic, or attempting to kill the snake. And all of this is based on a simple misconception. In the same way, we mistakenly believe that our body and mind possess a sort of self from which all our other problems come, like desire and anger. And on the basis of this self-centered attitude, and of our misconceived self, we distinguish between "I" and "other."

~

Everything is interdependent

Were there something partless, it might be independent, but there is nothing that is partless. Rather, everything exists in dependence on its parts, and is only designated in dependence on its parts through conceptual thinking. If things did in fact exist the way they appear, then when one investigated them, this inherent existence should become even clearer and more obvious. But experience shows that when we search for these things analytically, we cannot find them. For instance, conventionally there is an "I" undergoing pleasure and pain, accumulating *karma* and so forth, but

~

when we search for this "I" through analysis, we cannot find it. There is no whole which is separate from its parts. Thus, phenomena are said to be illusions.

~

The nature of the mind

In order to prove that enlightenment is possible, we base our argument on the fact that the nature of the mind is sheer luminosity and awareness. This means that enlightenment is attained by knowing the true nature of the mind.

If the mental poisons – attachment, hatred, and ignorance – were inherent to the nature of our mind, then it would be impossible to counteract them for this would mean that hatred, for example, would be constantly present in us. It would only dissolve when our consciousness dissolved, which

~

clearly is not the case. This proves that the nature of the mind is not sullied by the defects of the poisons, and therefore there is nothing to prevent us from eradicating them altogether since they are distinct from primordial consciousness.

~

Who created the universe?

If evolution has a cause, there are two possible explanations for it. You could accept that the universe was created by God, but this will entail many contradictions such as that suffering and evil were also necessarily created by God. The other possibility is to say that there are an infinite number of living beings whose karmic potential has collectively created the whole of this universe, as a fitting environment. The universe in which we live is created by our own aspirations and actions. At least this argument has the advantage of being logical.

~

Space and the big bang

Many Eastern philosophers, and Buddhists in particular, speak of the four elements of earth, water, fire, and air, to which space is added as a fifth element. The first four elements exist thanks to the fifth one, space, which allows them to manifest and function.

According to certain Buddhist texts like the Kalachakra Tantra, space or ether is not a total void or nothingness. It is composed of "emptiness particles." The four elements arise from these emptiness particles, going from the subtlest matter to gross matter (air, fire, water, and earth), and this process is called generation. Then they dissolve back, from gross matter to subtle matter, and dissolve into emptiness particles, and this process is called dissolution. Space, or universal emptiness, is the basis of the entire process.

The big-bang theory on the birth of the universe definitely has some common ground with universal emptiness. The subtlest particles studied in modern physics seem to be quite similar to what we call emptiness particles. This is why I think it is very important to reflect on these similarities.

~

The origin of the universe

Buddhists assert that the century in which we are living now is a result of the centuries that preceded it, and so on, until the beginning of time some 20 or 25 billion years ago. But why and how did the big bang occur? Nobody can explain that. There are two explanations that I find personally unacceptable. According to the first one, nothing has a cause. Things happen just like that, of themselves. From our point of view that is untenable. In Buddhism, all events must have a cause. The second explanation is the divine solution: one day, God decided to create the world. We do not

~

accept this either. Our scriptures assert that subtle particles existed in space before the creation of the universe. And they are still there. So is it these spiritual particles that compose beings that produced the big bang? Then why? And how? We believe that any single universe can exist and then disintegrate, and immense cycles of time can elapse in the process. But the universe as a whole – the universal "spirit" – is always there. One might even imagine that this subtle spirit, which has incomparable power, is the primary principle of creation. Maybe at some point certain beings were delighted by the existence of this universe and that is why it exists.

~

"Form is emptiness, emptiness is form"

We are empty, or rather the matter of which we are composed is empty. But I must emphasize that emptiness does not mean nothingness. Some commentators have been mistaken when they have accused Buddhism of being nihilistic. We believe that the world in which we live is part of a flux, a stream of events. This does not mean it is nothing. Everything depends on everything else. Nothing exists on its own. On account of all the influences that come to bear upon them, things appear, exist, and disappear, and then reappear again. But they never exist independently. Form is therefore

~

empty, by which we mean it is not separate and independent. Form depends on a multitude of different factors. And emptiness is form because all forms emerge from emptiness, from this absence of independent existence. Emptiness exists only to give rise to form.

~

Emptiness is like the idea of zero

Emptiness corresponds to the idea of zero, to the total absence of intrinsic existence. A zero, in itself, is nothing, yet without zero counting is impossible. Therefore zero is something and nothing at the same time. The same goes for emptiness. Emptiness is empty, and at the same time it is the basis of everything.

~

The direct approach

Conceptual thought has its limitations, as we all know. That is why most traditions have tried to find a "direct" approach on the difficult path to knowledge. Mysticism, yoga, certain types of meditation, and ecstasy are all included in this direct approach, which leads to awakening. According to Tibetan tradition, the direct approach can take us experientially all the way to the origin of the world, but it is extremely difficult. It assumes the highest and subtlest degree of mental development and refinement, such that the mind is free of the cycle of time. I have friends who are still living and who have experienced such moments.

~

Science and moral consciousness

Scientific research is based on experimentation with the aid of specific instruments. Spiritual research relies on inner experience and meditation. We should make a clear distinction between what has not been discovered by science, and what has been scientifically discovered to be non-existent. Clearly, there are still many mysteries. The human senses can perceive the world to a certain extent, but we cannot assert that there is nothing beyond what we can access through our five senses. As for the moral consciousness, although human beings have experienced this for centuries, we are still

~

not sure what it really is or how it works. What it perceives has no form and no color, and belongs to a category of phenomena that cannot be apprehended by means of the methods we use to examine external things.

~

Death and clear light

Death will definitely come. If you spend your life overly concerned with just the temporary affairs of this lifetime, and make no preparation for it, then on the day when it comes you will be unable to think about anything except your own mental suffering and fear, and will have no opportunity to practice anything else.

When death is near, it is essential to turn your thoughts to spiritual practice, since the mind at the time of dying is a proximate cause of the continuation into the next lifetime. No matter what

~

has happened in terms of good and bad within this particular lifetime, what happens at the time of death is particularly powerful. Therefore it is important to learn about the process of dying and prepare for it through meditation. I do this myself. Six or seven times a day, I go through the eight phases of dissolution that occur at death in my meditation practice.

The process begins with the dissolution of the *aggregate* of forms. In rough terms, when the aggregate of forms begins to disintegrate, this means that the earth constituent is losing its force in the sense of becoming less capable of serving

~

as a basis of consciousness. Simultaneously with this, the capacity of the water constituent in your body to serve as a basis of consciousness becomes more manifest. As an external sign of this, your limbs become thinner, more frail, and the freshness of your appearance deteriorates. You have the sense that your body is sinking under the ground, and your eyesight becomes unclear. As an internal sign, you have the inner experience of seeing a mirage.

After that, in the second stage, the aggregate of feelings dissolves. At that time, the water constituent decreases in force in terms of its capacity to act as a basis of consciousness, due to which the capacity of the fire constituent becomes more manifest. As external signs, the fluids of the body dry up, and your eyes move less. Internally, the sign of this stage is that you have a sense of seeing an appearance of smoke.

In the third stage the aggregate of discriminations dissolves, at which time the fire constituent lessens in force in the sense that it is less able to serve as a basis of consciousness, the wind constituent thereby becoming manifest in terms of this capacity. As an external sign, your sense of heat diminishes, and your memory of loved ones deteriorates.

As an internal sign you have a sense of an appearance of fireflies or scattering sparks.

In the fourth stage the aggregate of compositional factors dissolves, at which time the capacity of the wind constituent to act as a basis of consciousness weakens. As an external sign, your breath ceases. As an internal sign, you have a sense of a burning, reddish glow from a flame. In general, people consider this to be death because your heart is no longer beating and you are no longer breathing. If a doctor came, he would say you were already dead; however, from our point of view, you are still in the process of dying; you have not yet died. Your

~

sense consciousnesses have disappeared, but the mental consciousness remains. However, this does not mean that you could revive.

There are four levels of grossness and subtlety within the mind that remains, and thus there are four further stages of dissolution of the elements. The coarse begin to dissolve first. With the first, the internal sign is that a white appearance dawns; this is the mind of radiant white appearance. It is compared to a clear autumn sky filled with just moonlight. There are no more external signs.

~

When the mind of radiant white appearance dissolves together with the wind or energy that serves as its mount, a more subtle mind appears called the mind of radiant red increase. It is compared to a clear autumn sky filled with just reddish or orange sunlight.

When the mind of radiant red increase dissolves along with its mount, a still more subtle mind appears, the mind of radiant black near-attainment. It is compared to the complete darkness of a clear autumn sky in the first period of the night. During the initial part of this level of mind, you are still aware, but then the capacity for conscious

~

awareness deteriorates, and you become as if unconscious.

When the mind of radiant black near-attainment dissolves together with the wind that serves as its mount, the most subtle of all minds appears – the clear light of death, actual death. It is compared to an immaculate dawn sky in autumn, without any other appearance. The mind of clear light is called the fundamental mind because it is the root of all minds. It is this mind that exists beginninglessly and continuously in each individual through each lifetime and into buddhahood.

~

This is when life really stops. For ordinary mortals it is a moment of unconsciousness or fainting. For a yogi, the time has come to put his or her practice to the test before the cells degenerate. This is when you come to know the subtlest level of all: awareness of clear light.

~

The three levels of consciousness

According to its level of subtlety, consciousness is classified into three levels: the waking state or gross level of consciousness; the consciousness of the dream state, which is more subtle; and the consciousness during dreamless sleep, which is subtler still. Similarly, the three stages of birth, death, and the intermediate state of the *bardo* are also established in terms of the subtlety of their levels of consciousness.

During the death process, one penetrates to the deepest level of the subtle consciousness. But after

~

death, in the intermediate state, one is drawn by one's future rebirth and the consciousness again becomes more gross. It gradually becomes more and more gross through rebirth and reincarnation.

There is a considerable amount of documentation presenting cases of people who remember their past lives. It would be beneficial to research this area in order to further human knowledge.

~

The Buddhist theory of cause and effect

If you want to know what you were doing in the past, look at your body now. If you want to know what will happen to you in the future, look into what your mind is doing now.

Pleasure and pain are effects. The fact that they change shows that they depend on causes. This is why you will not experience the pleasure you want unless you create its causes, and you will prevent the suffering that you want to avoid by giving up its causes. As soon as a cause of suffering is inscribed in your mental continuum, you will have to go

~

through its effects whether or not you would prefer to avoid suffering.

The effect of harmful actions is based on the intensity of the delusions that motivate them. It also corresponds to the associated cause. By way of an example, consider that even after you have taken rebirth in a lower realm as a result of killing, if you then succeed in gaining a human rebirth it will be short-lived. The effect of stealing means that one will not enjoy material comforts, and the effect of sexual misconduct entails a faithless partner. If you have offended people you will be subject to insult, and if you have stirred up

~

ill-feeling within a family or community the effect is that your friends will fall out with you; and so on. As for wrong views, they result in a lack of protection with nowhere to take refuge. Our present happiness, or our present unhappiness, are nothing other than the result of past actions.

~

The key to good fortune
and to misfortune

There are innumerable differences within the human family. Some people are always successful, while for others it is the exact opposite. In spite of what others might expect, certain people are prone to misfortune while others, about whom we might expect the worst, are free of it. Reflecting on this, we can see to what extent life is beyond our control. We might do our level best and bring together all the keys for success, and yet fail to achieve our goal. It is said that some are lucky and others unlucky, but this explanation is unsatisfactory.

~

There must be a reason for this good fortune, there must be a cause behind it. Buddhism explains that it is the result of actions committed either in previous lives or in our earlier life.

~

The effects of individuals
on the environment

We could say that, in general, the evolution of the universe is linked to the karma of beings. This is quite a complex matter, but let's take the example of climate change. Imagine a community that is dominated by hatred and anger. I think that this sort of negative emotion could have an impact on their environment, and could contribute to producing a heat wave or drought. If we imagine another group in which attachment and covetousness are very strong and widespread, this might be the cause of high rainfall and floods. I am only

~

considering these possibilities, I am not saying anything definitive here. But whether it be on an individual or a community level, there is no doubt that the actions of each one of us, the behavior and mood we have day after day, month after month, and year after year, will have an influence on the collective environment.

~

Serenity comes through Buddhist practice

Our belief in life after death helps to bring about a certain serenity regarding our personal development, as well as an acceptance of everything as it arises. We know that it is useless to give in to agitation, or to worry about our suffering. Perceiving the transitory nature of suffering more and more clearly does not lead to apathy, or to the sense that nothing matters. Rather, we recognize suffering for what it is and attribute to this recognition the power of generating the aspiration to be free of suffering altogether.

~

The Four Noble Truths

The Buddha said, "This is true suffering, this is its true cause, this is its true cessation, this is the true path." He also said, "Know suffering, renounce its causes, attain the cessation of suffering, and follow the true path." And again, he said, "Know suffering, even though there is nothing to know; abandon the causes of suffering, even though there is nothing to abandon; apply yourself diligently to renunciation, even though there is nothing to renounce; and practice the means of attainment, even though there is nothing to practice." These are the three aspects of the ground, path, and ultimate result of the Four Noble Truths.

~

GLOSSARY

AGGREGATES

The principal faculties which constitute a sentient being, namely form, feeling, perception/discrimination, conditioning/motivational factors, and consciousness.

AHIMSA

Ethical principle of non-violence.

~

AVALOKITESHVARA

An embodiment of the compassion of all the buddhas, visualized in the form of a meditational deity. Avalokiteshvara (Tib. Chenrizig) is considered to be the patron deity of Tibet.

BARDO

The interval or intermediate period of experience between death and rebirth.

BODHICITTA

An altruistic aspiration to attain full enlightenment for the benefit of all beings. Literally, "bodhi" means enlightenment and "citta" means mind.

~

BODHISATTVA

A spiritual trainee who has generated the altruistic mind of bodhicitta and is on the path to full enlightenment. Bodhisattvas are courageous individuals who dedicate their entire being towards a single goal: to bring about the welfare of all sentient beings.

BUDDHA

Buddha literally means "awakened," "developed," and "enlightened." A buddha is a fully awakened being who, as a result of training the mind through the spiritual paths, has finally reached the full potential for complete enlightenment and has eliminated all the obstructions to knowledge.

~

DHARMA

Dharma refers to the teachings of Buddhism.

EMPTINESS

The ultimate nature of reality, which is the total absence of inherent existence and self-identity with respect to all phenomena.

GAUTAMA

The family name ascribed to the historical Buddha, Shakyamuni, in the ancient texts.

GURU

A Sanskrit word for the spiritual teacher or mentor. The Tibetan equivalent is "lama."

~

HINAYANA

One of the two main systems or "vehicles" of Buddhism, emphasizing an individual's liberation from samsara, or cyclic existence. This is also known as Vipassana.

KANGYUR

The Tibetan Buddhist canon which contains a large number of original scriptures translated from Indian sources.

KARMA

The doctrine of actions and their causal consequences.

~

KATA

A white silk scarf traditionally given as a greeting.

LAMA

Tibetan term for the spiritual teacher or mentor.

MAHAYANA

One of the two main systems or "vehicles" of Buddhism, emphasizing complete liberation from the various delusions and misconceptions concerning phenomenal existence, as well as the motivation of altruism, with the liberation of others as the principal objective.

~

MANTRA

A specific practice in spiritual training that protects the mind from the overwhelming influence of ordinary perceptions and conceptions.

MARA

The personification of the forces of ignorance.

NIRVANA

The permanent cessation of all suffering, and the afflictive emotions which cause and perpetuate suffering. It is the extinction of all our misconceptions, afflictive emotions, and negative tendencies within the ultimate sphere of emptiness.

SAMSARA

A state of existence, conditioned by one's karmic tendencies and imprints from past actions, which is characterized by a cycle of life and death and by suffering.

SANGHA

This traditionally refers to the spiritual communities of ordained practitioners, that is, of Buddhist monks and nuns.

SENTIENT BEINGS

A technical term denoting beings in cyclic existence, and distinguishing them from fully enlightened buddhas.

~

SHAKYAMUNI

Name of the historical Buddha, indicating that he was born into the Shakya clan.

SHANTIDEVA

A great bodhisattva of classical India, especially noted for his works on the essential qualities of a bodhisattva's conduct.

SIX PERFECTIONS

The spiritual practice of a bodhisattva is categorized into six perfections: generosity, discipline, patience, effort, meditative concentration, and wisdom.

~

SUTRA

The original discourses which Buddha Shakyamuni taught to his disciples.

TATHAGATAGARBHA

The seed of buddhahood, or buddha nature, present but uncultivated in the mental continuum of all sentient beings, and without which the attainment of enlightenment or buddhahood would be impossible.

THE THREE JEWELS

The Three Jewels consist of the Buddha, the Dharma, and the Sangha. Taking Refuge in the

~

Three Jewels means entrusting one's spiritual growth and wellbeing to them, and is the mark of becoming a practicing Buddhist.

~

Selected works by the Dalai Lama

My Land and My People, McGraw-Hill, New
   York, 1977.

Kindness, Clarity and Insight, transl. and ed.
   J. Hopkins, Snow Lion, Ithaca, 1984.

The Meaning of Life from a Buddhist perspective, ed.
   J. Hopkins, Wisdom Publications, Boston, 1992.

*A Flash of Lightning in the Dark of Night: A guide
   to the bodhisattva's way of life*, Padmakara
   translation Group, Shambhala, 1994.

The World of Tibetan Buddhism, transl. and ed.
   Geshe Thupten Jinpa, Wisdom Publications,
   Boston, 1995.